The Gate of Hope

PINNACLE
BOOKS

Published by PINNACLE BOOKS
P.O. Box 737
Liberty, Missouri 64068
Edited by Marian Fuller
Cover by Sandra L. Wilkes
Manufactured in the United States of America

LIBRARY OF CONGRESS CATALOGING IN PUBLICATION DATA
Morgan, Charles Robert
    The Gate of Hope

    Bibliography: p. 213
    Includes index.
    1. Bible, O.T. History – Exile to Jewish War.   2. Dead
Sea Scrolls – Intertestimental Period.   3. Bible. Gospels –
N.T. Criticism.   4. Jesus, Historical – Documentary hy-
pothesis.   5. Josephus – The Jewish War.   6. Hellenization,
O.T. & N.T. – Greco-Roman Culture.
I. Title.
ISBN 0-922753-00-8
Library of Congress Catalog Card Number: 88-063172

"In recent years, several publications dealing with the life of Christ have appeared. They have attracted a good deal of attention although some of them are not from the pens of professional Biblical specialists. We cannot merely disregard them, as some of them provide us with thoroughly prepared collections of material while also presenting us with a reliable assessment of the opinions of the specialists. These publications have not actually produced any new facts, although they have sometimes shed new light on already published material. Yet, in fact, this new light is not really new, for these views have for long been under discussion among the experts. The public has been made aware of these questions, however, by these publications and this is sufficient reason for not neglecting them."

Dr. Werner Keller

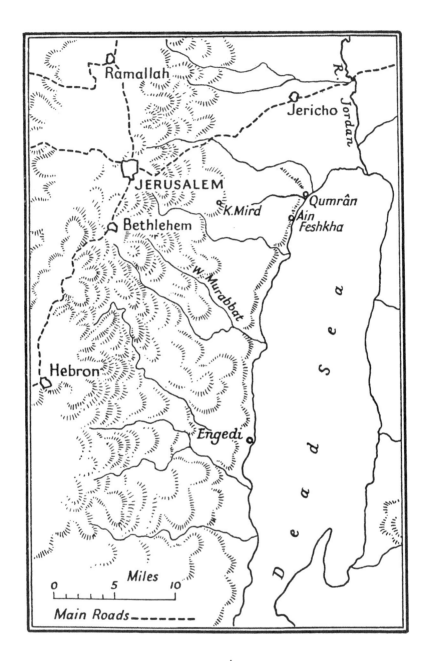

Ramallah

Jericho

R. Jordan

JERUSALEM

K.Mird

Qumrân

Ain Feshkha

Bethlehem

W. Murabbat

Hebron

Engedi

Dead Sea

Miles

0   5   10

Main Roads - - - - - - -

iv

"I Jesus have sent my angel to you with this testimony for the churches. I am the root and the offspring of David, the bright morning star."
(Revelation 22:16)

"May God bless thee with all good and keep thee from all evil, and illumine thy heart with insight into the things of life, and grace thee with knowledge of things eternal, and lift up His gracious countenance towards thee to grant thee peace everlasting."
(The Manual of Discipline)

The
Gate of
Hope

C.R. Morgan

Preface

El Al flight 001 touched down in Tel Aviv at Ben Gurion airport uneventfully. I passed customs, and walked to the car rentals located in a building in front of the terminal. The trip to Jerusalem takes 40 minutes. I drove through the city to re-acquaint myself before I checked into my hotel. My plan was to dine and retire to get an early start in the morning. I awoke refreshed and looked at my watch. Local time was 2 a.m. As I contemplated waiting several hours in the room, a quiet excitement began to build. I found myself dressed and driving out of Jerusalem in just a few minutes.

The drive to the Dead Sea and Jordan River valley is not a difficult one; it's approximately 15 miles, just a 30-minute drive. The highway winds through the mountains just east of Jerusalem and emerges in the desert. I drove along the Dead Sea and turned off the main highway at Wady Qumran. The drive leads up to a terrace at the foot of a high mountain range that overlooks the sea. I could see the ancient ruins in the moonlight as I stopped to get out of the car.

It was a clear, still evening – the temperature lingered in the 80s. My watch read a few minutes after 3 a.m. I noticed another vehicle leave the highway and watched it climb up the same drive to the terrace. Two Israeli soldiers jumped out of their jeep, their

M-16s pointed at me. A challenge came in Arabic. As they approached, they saw the large white rental sign printed in big block letters on the automobile. The questioning then came in English. After a few minutes they were convinced I did not present any threat. The jeep left Qumran and did not return again that night.

There are no lights in the desert and this makes the stars seem a little brighter – a little closer. The limestone cliff which hangs over Khirbet Qumran is awesome during the day but in the moonlight it gave me a feeling of a strange presence. It was beautiful on the plateau among the palms overlooking the moon's reflection on the water. I walked into the ruins and sat down to stare at the stars.

Slowly, the sky began to change. It brightened behind the Mountains of Moab on the far side of the sea. The stars overhead were still brilliant, but those in the lower eastern sky began to fade. I remembered those who had once stood at this very place and performed this same ritual. The sky brightened more as the sun's glow rose slowly on the horizon. Now almost every star overhead became invisible. I watched as the long shadow of the mountains began to recede across the sea. I turned to watch the cliffs behind me. Light fell on the wady and the sun's first rays beamed onto the Gate.

Introduction

Forty years ago a most remarkable archaeological discovery
was made. In the spring of 1947, an Arab shepherd found the first
of a treasure of documents in a cave situated near the northwestern shore of the Dead Sea. This cave near the Wady Qumran,
was identified and subsequently excavated by an expedition
jointly undertaken by the Department of Antiquities of Jordan,
the Palestine Archaeological Museum and the Ecole Biblique beginning in 1949. In 1951 representatives of these same institutions returned to Qumran and made soundings which revealed
pottery identical with that which had been discovered in the first
caves, and coins which established the approximate date of the
ruin's occupation. It was decided to complete an excavation of
Qumran and four further excavations were made from 1953 to
1956. Further caves were explored and more important manuscripts were discovered.

All these discoveries have aroused enormous interest and it
is reasonable that this interest should be concentrated on these
texts. The archaeologists can make a contribution to the understanding of the texts by indicating the nature of the setting in
which they were discovered and so perhaps make it possible to
reconstruct the character of the group from which they emerged.
The historian strives for a historical explanation of the archaeo-

logical findings to establish the extent to which they can throw light upon the interpretation of the texts. The theologian offers a textual criticism through comparative literature of the books in the Old and New Testaments. Together, these disciplines combine to bring us an understanding of the documents and the community that conceived them.

This community, the life which has been traced by archaeologists over a period of some centuries, and which has left behind a considerable amount of literature, is no small unknown sect. It must belong to one of the movements which were important and well known within Judaism. The people of Qumran could not have been assimilated either to the Zealots, the Sadducees or the Pharisees. The community consisted of a people known as the Essenes who, according to the historian Pliny, lived precisely in this area.

The Essenes existed during the centuries just before the emergence of Christianity. They were organized in ways that suggest a relationship upon which Christian writers drew in composing their own scriptures. Theologians insist on the importance of the Old Testament for the understanding of the New. The Dead Sea Scrolls show that the legacy of Judaism is much richer, with ideas much wider, than had previosly been supposed. The Essenes had practices, including sacraments, which were forerunners of Christian practices. The community anticipated the coming of the Messiah.

The community at Qumran separated from Jerusalem and its priesthood which, in their eyes, had prevaricated. They were the converts of Israel who went from the "Land of Judah" and were exiled to the "Land of Damascus." This place of exile became a refuge where the faithful were saved from the anger of God. The exiles were the true remnant of Israel, and it is with them that God sealed a new covenant. The community called itself "the Remnant of Israel," "the True Israel," "the New Covenant."

Table of Contents

1

The Dead Sea Scrolls

Traveling down the last few miles of the River Jordan before it flows into the Dead Sea, one cannot help being overcome by awe at the natural features of this remarkable stretch of country. The valley which lies in the harshest desert on earth is nearly 1,300 feet below sea level, making it the lowest point on earth. A few miles north, Joshua led the Israelites across the Jordan into the Promised Land and after his formidable seven-day preparation defeated the inhabitants of Jericho. Elijah crossed back over the Jordan at this point during the last hours of his life, when "a chariot of fire" appeared and he "went up by a whirlwind into heaven."

Just north of the Dead Sea, John the Baptist prepared the way of the Lord and called for penitents to be baptized. Beyond Jericho, the Mount of Temptation extends between Jerusalem and the Jordan Valley. To the east lies the gracious Mountains of Moab. Jerusalem lies 15 miles west. To the south, along the eastern shore of the Dead Sea, lie the caves of Engedi. King Saul took 3,000 chosen men and went to seek David "upon the rocks of the wild goats" and instead of finding him, Saul actually set up his headquarters in the same cave where David was hiding.

The Wady[1] Qumran flows into the Dead Sea on the northwestern side. Two miles west of this point towers a limestone

1

cliff, 1,100 feet high. A close look reveals that the cliff is honeycombed with innumerable natural caves. It was in one of these caves that an Arab shepherd quite accidentally made the most fabulous archaeological discovery of all time.

Muhammed the Wolf, a young Bedouin of the Ta'amireh tribe, discovered Cave I in the spring of 1947. Muhammed was looking after his goats under the high cliffs on the western shore when one of the goats strayed up the craggy rocks. As he went up after the goat, Muhammed noticed an odd shaped hole in the cliff. He picked up a rock and threw it in. He listened for the thud of the rock, but instead heard the sound of a breaking jar. The young boy was too afraid to enter the cave alone and so he returned home.

The next day he came back to investigate with an older friend. They squeezed through the hole to explore the cave. Inside they found several large clay jars in rows against the wall on the floor. They became very excited and hoped that the jars would hold some treasure of gold. Their findings brought them disappointment. Had they known it, the contents were more valuable than gold.

The jars that were still intact were tightly sealed, and the Bedouins, hoping for treasure, hastened to open them. They were unable to recognize at first the contents, except that they were more or less cylindrical objects, partly decayed with a disagreeable odor. Upon closer inspection the cylinders turned out to be manuscripts tightly rolled and written in a language the Bedouins believed to be Syriac. Of the 40 jars that once stood in the cave, only two were recovered intact, the rest smashed by the Bedouins or others in their haste to get at the contents.

The Ta'amireh tribe is a nomadic tribe. Many were smugglers of contraband across the troubled frontier. Some engaged in highway robbery not unlike the thieves who beat up the traveller in the Parable of the Good Samaritan. Believing the manuscripts to have some value, the Ta'amireh carried them on their journey across the desert for Bethlehem to transact their deals on the black market. When they arrived in Bethlehem, they sold three of the scrolls to a dealer named Kando[2] for 20 pounds.

Kando was not impressed and they laid in his shop for several days until he showed them to the Syrian metropolitan at the Monastery of St. Mark.[3] Needless to say, when the metropolitan, Athanasius Yeshue Samuel, saw the scrolls, he was very interested indeed. He recognized the language in which they were written as being Hebrew and knew there was probably a good chance of finding more documents since no one had lived near Wady Qumran for nearly 2,000 years. He tried to buy more scrolls but the Bedouin had already departed on another journey. After they received a message and returned to St. Mark's, they were mistaken for street vendors and turned away. The metropolitan finally caught up with them and managed to purchase five more of the scrolls for 50 pounds. This purchase was not made public because all antiquities discovered must be reported to the authorities and these actions by the Bedouin were illegal.

Meanwhile, a black market trader in November 1947, who referred to himself as "a dealer of antiquities," called on Dr. E. L. Sukenik,[4] professor of Archaeology, at Hebrew University. He presented fragments from some manuscripts found in a cave near the Dead Sea that a dealer in Bethlehem was prepared to sell. This happened to occur at the time when Great Britain surrendered the mandate over to Palestine and the United Nations passed the resolution to partition Palestine. There was fighting between Arabs and Jews. A journey to Bethlehem would be extremely dangerous. The entry in his diary dated Dec. 1, 1947, reads: "I read a little more in the parchments. I'm afraid of going too far in thinking about them. It may be that this is one of the greatest finds ever made in Palestine, a find we never so much hoped for."[5]

Sukenik carried out his mission successfully. He held a press conference after his return to Jerusalem. The reporters who showed up were nervous due to the shells of the Arab Legion exploding around them. His eagerness and enthusiasm to tell the world about this discovery made Sukenik impervi-

3

ous to the danger.

In February 1948, the metropolitan had contacted the American School of Oriental Research. The scrolls were turned over to Acting Director Dr. John Trevor, since Director Miller Burrows was away in Iraq. Trevor compared the scrolls to early Hebrew manuscripts; the scrolls were much older. He compared the scrolls to slides of the Nash Papyrus which is at the University Library at Cambridge and dated 200 B.C. to A.D. 100. There was a striking resemblance. Trevor worked with the metropolitan to take pictures of the scrolls which he then sent to Professor Dr. Albright of John Hopkins University. By the time Burrows had returned from his trip, a letter arrived from Albright: "My heartiest congratulations on the greatest manuscript discovery of modern times! There is no doubt in my mind that the script is more archaic than that of the Nash Papyrus...What an absolutely incredible find!"

The Americans were anxious to visit the cave but the situation in Palestine was deteriorating. It was clear that when the British mandate expired on May 14, a full scale civil war would break out. Expecting pending chaos, the metropolitan sent the scrolls out of the country at the advice of Burrows.

Almost immediately Professor Yigael Yadin of the University of Jerusalem, arranged for the purchase of the scrolls on behalf of the Israeli government, the price being some 1,500 times what the metropolitan had paid. The Israeli government placed the scrolls along with those purchased by Sukenik in the "Shrine of Books," built in the Israeli section of Jerusalem.

Many more scrolls and fragments were still to be found, but these original seven found in Cave I are what were originally referred to as the Dead Sea Scrolls. The largest and most impressive is the St. Mark Isaiah Scroll, so-called because the metropolitan kept it at St. Mark's Monastery before sending it out of Palestine. It is 24 feet long, 10 inches wide, consists of 17 strips of sheepskin and is divided into 54 columns. The scroll is the complete text of Isaiah and confirms the accuracy of the Massoretic texts.

The second Isaiah Scroll was part of Sukenik's purchase. It contains chapters 38 to the end.

The third scroll is the Habakkuk Commentary, which consists of 13 columns on two pieces of leather sewn together. It is 5 feet long and 5 1/2 inches wide. It reinterprets the prophecies of Habakkuk, the prophet who has always been considered obscure, and the commentary is even more obscure.

The fourth and fifth scrolls are The War Between the Sons of Light and the Sons of Darkness, and The Thanksgiving Hymns. The War Scroll is just over 9 feet long and measures 6 inches wide. It is in good condition and describes in military detail the part to be played by the Community in the final battle between God and Belial, in which the Sons of Light destroy the Sons of Darkness. The Hymns Scroll was in two separate parts with about 20 Psalms. They present the theology of the Community in prayer form.

The Manual of Discipline gives more information than any other scroll about the life of the Essene Community. It is 6 feet long and 10 inches wide.

The last is the Genesis Apocryphon Scroll, 9 feet long by 12 inches wide. It is a pseudepigraphic narration by Abraham of many of the events in the Book of Genesis.

On May 29, 1948, the U.N. Security Council declared a cease-fire and ordered all fighting to stop. The country was divided along borders describing territories for the Arabs and Israelis. Jordan included more than half of Jerusalem, including nearly all of the Old City. It also included Bethlehem, and the larger part of the Dead Sea, including the Wady Qumran. All the discoveries at Qumran lay within the province and jurisdiction of the director of the Jordanian Department of Antiquities, G. Lankester Harding.

Harding served the Commonwealth with integrity and unselfishness, and had worked for several different countries with complete devotion. It was necessary for Harding to rediscover Cave I to see if any archaeological evidence remained. When he tried to pinpoint the source of the scrolls, he was faced with an awkward problem. The scrolls provided the Ta'amireh tribe with a profitable venture. They had made a considerable amount of money on the early caves alone. With the help of a detachment of troops, and knowing the approximate location, he was able to locate Cave I.

From this point Harding worked with Père Roland de Vaux, of the Ecole Biblique.[6] Harding and de Vaux spent a month at Qumran in February 1949. They assured themselves that this was Cave I and in spite of the archaeological damage by illicit excavators, managed to collect a large number of scroll fragments. It was apparent by the number of broken jar fragments that the Bedouin probably possessed large numbers of fragments and quite possibly some entire scrolls. They would have to be alert to buy these back as they surfaced on the black market.

Harding announced that the authorities would buy manuscripts at a good price with no questions asked. It took many weeks of patient negotiation to instill confidence with the Arabs. Finally, Harding met the two boys who had made the original discovery. He sent them back to their tribe well rewarded and with a tale that here was an English official who could speak their tongue and who knew their customs better than any foreigner they had ever met.

Late in 1951, the Ta'amireh brought Harding more samples. They were persuaded to lead Harding and de Vaux to Wady Murabba'at, a point 10 miles south of Wady Qumran. Four caves on the steep cliff revealed some objects of the Bronze and Iron Ages and more biblical and non-biblical manuscripts.

Harding and de Vaux were sorting through their finds when they received word the Bedouin had taken up archaeology. Since the price for one square centimeter was one pound, the tribal chiefs had assumed the role of personnel directors of their amateur speleologists. With the difficulty of the terrain and thousands of caves to be searched, Harding had no choice but to use the Bedouin. No one knew the ground as well but there were many drawbacks. The Bedouin concealed their best finds and much damage was done in their hasty enthusiasm.

6

Harding wanted to curtail the damage being done. He tried to have the Bedouin rounded up by government troops but they disappeared into the hills returning later to sell their finds. Harding called on help from American and French schools of archaeology. Under the leadership of de Vaux, over 200 caves were searched. In only two, Cave II and III, was any valuable material found.

In 1952, the Ta'amireh were excelling themselves. They were removing vast numbers of fragments from other caves when the greatest discovery of all was made in what would later be known as Cave IV, "The Partridge Cave." One evening, an old man of the Ta'amireh tribe recalled that, when he was out hunting as a youth, he had followed a wounded partridge into a peculiar hole near the Qumran ruins. He had entered into the cave and discovered an old lamp and some potsherds. The old man was able to recall a good description of the place — good enough to lead the young members of his audience to it without difficulty. With the use of ropes and lamps they came upon a vast store of documents. This was the discovery of the Qumran library.

Cave IV contained the fragments of 400 manuscripts, most of which had to be purchased from the Bedouin. It became clear to Harding and de Vaux that they did not have the resources to cope with so enormous a find. To the credit of Jordan, the government appropriated 15,000 pounds to preserve the Qumran library at a time when it was pressed by demands for defense and social welfare.[7] Every small fragment had to be collected in case it might be the key to the jigsaw of a page.

An international team of scholars was assembled for the purpose of piecing the giant jigsaw together at the Palestine Museum in the Jordanian sector of Jerusalem. The team was composed of: P.W. Skehan, professor at Catholic University of America; F.M. Cross, professor at the Divinity School, Harvard; J.T. Millik, Father Maurice Baillet and J. Starcky, all three associated with the Center of Scientific Research in Paris; John Strugnell of Jesus College, Oxford; J.M. Allegro of Manchester University; and C.H. Huntzinger, of the University of Göttingen.[8]

By 1956 all the material contained in Cave IV had been recovered but the process of piecing it together taxed the team's ingenuity for the following two years. In the meantime, the Ta'amireh discovered Caves V to XI. Only Cave XI can be compared to Cave I and Cave IV. A few of its treasures include a psalter in good condition and the Book of Leviticus.

2

Khirbet Qumran

After a systematic search of the caves in the Wady Qumran region, attention was now turned one-half mile south to the ruins at Khirbet[1] Qumran. Occupants of the caves appeared likely to have been members of a group whose headquarters were the buildings represented by the ruins. Connected to them is a cemetery containing 1,200 graves.

In his *Naturalis Historia*, Pliny the Elder had described a monastery not far north of Engedi on the western shore of the Dead Sea. He called it the Essene monastery. Here the Essene community lived some way back from the shore for protection from the noxious effects of the water. Members of the community lived in isolation, with only palm trees for company. The Essene settlement, which was located on higher ground to the west, looked down on Engedi. Pliny was describing the location at Khirbet Qumran.

Although the buildings once on the site had been temporarily used as a Roman garrison, their original occupation was for a very different purpose. Professor A. Dupont-Sommer of the University of Paris was the first to hypothesize that the ruins had once been the Qumran monastery. It became known that one of the manuscripts[2] described the rules of the order for the community that could have been the one Pliny wrote about. Even though Jericho is only 7 miles north, and Jerusalem only 15 miles west, it is unlikely that the scrolls came from one of these cities. They had probably been placed in the caves by someone in the immediate vicinity.

Others joined Dupont-Sommer in calling for the excavation of the ruins. In 1951, Harding and de Vaux began the first systematic excavation. It corroborated Dupont-Sommer's surmise that Khirbet Qumran was the monastery in which the scrolls were written. The interpretation of the evidence presented is accepted by de Vaux, Milik, Burrows and Cross.

The ruins are quite unlike the typical Palestinian village. It was not a collection of separate families but a closely-knit community — a family with an admirable water supply, workshops for their activities, large assembly rooms and a remarkable cemetery.

The cemetery occupies two-thirds of the projecting terrace. Over 1,200 graves are dug in rows and contain the remains of unidentified corpses buried about four feet deep and partly covered with bricks of unbaked clay. The heads lie to the south, the hands folded over the waist. No gifts or jewels are buried with the bodies. Few of the graves are women's graves. In the main cemetery the skeletons are all of men. In two smaller cemeteries skeletons of women and children were found.

The buildings were separated from the cemetery by a strong wall on the east side. The main entrance was in the northwest. Here once stood an impressive tower with two or maybe even three floors. From the north runs an aqueduct, leading directly from a reservoir and originally a dam in the ravine above. Water and ablutions of a ceremonial kind were immensely important to the Community. There are six large cisterns connected by an elaborate system of canals. The complex of buildings to the west of the tower between the aqueduct and the ravine were storehouses. An oven and a corn mill were found. One small room contained three buried pots with 500 silver coins, all from the period before 9 B.C.

The main group of buildings lie east and south of the tower. There is a kitchen with several fireplaces, abutting the cemetery wall are a laundry and a latrine. Near the tower are a small room with a bench that runs along most of the walls and a courtyard with steps leading up one story to a scriptorium. Here the scribes sat before long narrow tables. Each scribe shared with his neighbor a small table on which was kept a supply of reed pens and cylindrical inkstands. The longest of these tables is now preserved in the Amman Museum. These remains were found on top of the collapsed ceiling of the room below. Two inkwells, one of bronze and the other of clay were also found. Many potsherds[3] were found on which the scribes used to practice their penmanship.

The largest room is the hall, 70 feet long by 14 feet wide. Here gatherings were held, and readings and commentaries on the Scriptures, as well as prayers and eating of sacred meals. Near the southwest corner of the hall is a circular, paved area that could have served as a type of pulpit or lectern. A small pantry is located next to the hall. In it are the pieces of pottery that had once been carefully stacked.

In vacant spaces between the buildings or round them the excavations have laid bare animal bones deposited between large sherds of pitchers or pots, or sometimes placed in jars left intact with their lids on. The bones are remnants of meals. Some of the meals seem to have had a religious significance. Most of the bones are clean but some have been charred, which shows that the meat was generally boiled and sometimes roasted. The care with which the bones were set apart after the flesh had been eaten reveals a religious preoccupation. It is possible that these are the remnants of sacrifices in which the victim was eaten by the faithful.

Through the laundry and the largest cistern runs a remarkable earthquake flaw. It runs the length of the buildings, and caused the east side to drop two feet. There are also traces of fire. The fire was probably a result of the earthquake in 31 B.C. and helps date the second occupation of the Qumran site. The site was unoccupied during most of the reign of Herod the Great.

In the southwest corner is a well-preserved potter's outfit — a basin for kneading the clay, a tank and two kilns. This

11

explained the jars in which the cave manuscripts had been hidden. The caves in the rock cliffs contained provision jars, pots, bowls, juglets and other domestic crockery. This indicated that from time to time these caves had become occupied. Huts and tents had also been set up at the foot of the rock cliffs of Qumran.[4]

The connections are well established between the buildings, scrolls and the Qumran caves. It is hardly conceivable that the same unusual pottery that was found in the caves should be the same as that in the ruins unless the two are connected. Paleographers proved that the writings on the potsherds found in the scriptorium were the same as the Hebrew writing of the scrolls. When the proximity of Cave IV to the buildings is considered, there can be no doubt as to their relationship.

Two miles south of Qumran, near the Spring of 'Ain Feshkha, another complex of buildings was excavated. Here a group of men and women lived to raise livestock and grow crops for the Community. They lived in a fairly large structure made up of a courtyard surrounded by small rooms for family living. The women could take care of their children and the small ones who had been adopted.

The connection between these and Qumran is taken as certain. The agricultural center was occupied during the same period — from the first century B.C. to A.D. 68 — with a similar gap in occupation during the reign of Herod the Great. Evidence of coins and pottery found there corroborates those like de Vaux and Milik who are convinced that all these buildings formed the Essene monastery. Remembering that there are several springs between Feshkha and Qumran, and that several charred trunks of palm trees have been found at Qumran, it is easy to understand how Pliny gave the community the pleasing name of "the Companies of the Palm Trees."

3

The Battle of the Scrolls

For Jews and Christians alike, there were certain questions round which the "Battle of the Scrolls" was fought. What were the dates of the documents? Who wrote them and for what purpose? These were important questions for paleographers and archaeologists, as well as for historians and theologians. Great interest was aroused by the accounts of a community which went into the wilderness to build a perfect society resembling in many ways the early Christian church, and which was founded by a Teacher of Righteousness.[1]

Albright confirmed in 1947 that one of the first scrolls from Cave I should be dated in the first century B.C. He described the manuscript discovery as the greatest of modern times. The revelation was so amazing that some scholars suspected forgery.

In the early days before the link was established between Khirbet and the caves, much had been written by authors who were later glad to retract their statements. Now that the dust has settled, a calm retrospect is possible. One must assess the various sciences which have made their own contribution with unexpected unanimity.

Paleography is the science and systematic study of ancient writings. It carefully compares the shape of each letter written in manuscripts of varying dates. The modifications of those shaped in the course of time are observable facts from which inferences can be drawn. This scientific discipline has become so exact that over a very large mass of material covering two to three centuries such as the material found at Qumran, skilled paleographers like Milik, Strugnell or Cross can attain a great degree of certainty.

When the scrolls were discovered, they were compared to ancient documents from the Codex in Leningrad of the 10th century A.D. back to the Nash Papyrus, which is dated 150 B.C. When the first scrolls were brought to Trevor and Burrows at the American School in Jerusalem, they saw the resemblance to the Nash Papyrus. On just the evidence they possessed at that time, they knew the scrolls had to fall between 200 B.C. and no later than A.D. 100.

Two indications lead to the early dating of the works. One is the use of "scriptio plena," meaning the employment of letters of the alphabet to indicate vowels. For example, in Hebrew the elimination of vowels and the use of only consonants can make translating very difficult (the word ld could mean lad, led, lid, lead, load, loud, aloud, lady or dozens of other words). The St. Mark Isaiah Scroll makes lavish use of the vowel letters, much before the text became standardized and before scriptio plena, which was most popular in the second century B.C., began to fall into disuse.

A second indication of early dating is the number of ligatures used. These connections between letters occur in Papyri of the fourth and third centuries B.C. and in the Nash Papyrus. After A.D. 100 their use is increasingly rare. Ligatures are frequent in the scrolls, especially in the Book of Isaiah.

Paleographical evidence has become very strong indeed, partly because of the quantity of the material from the caves and partly because of the skill and knowledge of the experts. Paleographers have learned to recognize the handwriting of many of the scribes and can identify the calligrapher from a small writing fragment. Some later texts found at Wady Murabba'at have the exact dates of the second century A.D. inscribed on them. They are written in a script a good deal later than the Qumran scrolls which confirms the accuracy of methods used by paleographical experts.

The books are written in four scripts: Phoenician, Square, Cursive and Mixed. Of the Square script there are four periods: the Archaic, ending about 150 B.C. in which copies of Samuel and Exodus from Cave IV were written; the Hasmonean from 150 to 50 B.C., in which a copy of the Book of Daniel was dated; the Herodian, from 50 B.C. to about A.D. 30, by which time the script had become most uniform; and the Ornamental, in which decorative curves appear. These are more common in latter documents found at Murabba'at.

The manuscripts found in Cave I were wrapped in decomposed clothes. The Carbon-14 test was used to help find the dates of these cloth wrappings. All living plants and animals absorb Carbon-14 until death when the process of disintegration begins at a constant rate. A radiation meter is used to measure the residue of carbon and from standard lapse rates the time disintegration began can be estimated, allowing for a small percent margin of error. The scroll cloths dated back to A.D. 33 with an allowable margin of error that would place the extreme limits for the date between 168 B.C. and A.D. 233. Although the wrappings may have been older or younger than the manuscripts they were wrapped around, it makes more sense to wrap an old manuscript with a new cloth than to wrap a new one with an old piece of cloth.

The pottery also tends to support a similar dating. All jars are of the same unusual kind. Two of the unbroken jars were recovered by Sukenik early in the proceedings. Thousands of pieces were collected and put on display in museums in Paris, Jerusalem, Chicago and Baltimore. Experts dated the two jars to be from 200 to 100 B.C. Two similar jars from Egypt belong to this same period. The jars probably were designed for other purposes than storing the scrolls. However, the custom of storing manuscripts in jars is attested to in the Book of Jeremiah, where instruction is given to put documents "in earthen vessels, that they may continue many days."

The origin of the jars was explained when an almost intact

15

potter's kiln was unearthed at Qumran. The Essene community was thought to be as self-supporting as possible, including their pottery. The clay came from deposits near the mouth of the Jordan. Many of the jars were fashioned on the potter's wheel at Qumran.

The ruins at Qumran had been noted for several hundred years by various travelers who had noticed Roman remains and had assumed that it once was a Roman fort. When serious excavations began, the archaeologists, headed by Cross were able to distinguish three periods of occupation. The first period, 1a,[2] consisted of temporary buildings and fixed the permanent plan which became the monastery. These were built over and covered by the main buildings in the second phase. Copper coins found in this strata date to the reign of John Hyrcanus I (134-104 B.C.). Since it takes time for coins to accumulate, and for historical reasons, Milik and others along with Cross believe the time of occupation to be closer to 160 B.C.

In period 1b,[3] the second phase of construction began about 125 B.C. when further building took place caused by an influx of Pharisees. Great numbers meant more building, a better water supply and the start of the agricultural settlement at 'Ain Feshkha. Many of the caves came into use. The Essenes flourished until the reign of Herod the Great, when buildings were destroyed by the earthquake of 31 B.C. The monastery was then unoccupied for about 30 years.

After the death of Herod, another emigration to the desert took place and Qumran once more was occupied. The reoccupation of Qumran in Period II[4] was accomplished no later than 1 B.C. – A.D. 1, when the same people returned. They continued their same way of life and the same industries were retained – the potter's workshop and the same ceramic tradition. Walls were built and biblical commentaries were written. The same special rites, as the burying of the bones, were continued. The pottery and coins are evidence to continuous occupation.

The occupation as a monastery ended during the third year

16

of the Jewish revolt.[5] The site became a Roman outpost to protect Jericho from the guerrillas of the south Judean desert. The main rooms were divided into barracks and the rest was left to fall further into ruin. The last bronze coins found were dated A.D. 68. Coins used as pay for Roman legionnaires minted in Caesara and Dara were found dated that same year.

Years later, partisans of Bar Kochebah occupied Qumran during the rebellion of A.D. 132 when he organized his resistance movement 10 miles south of Qumran. The site was not inhabited again until Harding and de Vaux pitched their tents in 1951.

4

Exile in Babylon

Since the time of Abraham, God has entered into a series of covenants with a peculiar group of people He has chosen to call His own. He has promised His blessings in return for faithful obedience. He has warned of His punishment if His people diluted their worship with idolatrous practices. Much of the Old Testament is about the Father grieving for His wayward and disobedient children. Finally, Israel's inequities were so great that God's wrath descended upon them.

The Northern Kingdom, Israel, in the eighth century B.C. was arrogant and prosperous. Instead of heeding the pleadings of the prophets Amos and Hosea, Israel fell victim to the Assyrian armies. In 721 B.C., Samaria, the capital, was subjugated and according to prevailing practice among ancient empires, the Assyrians deported the most capable people. Tens of thousands of people were violently driven from their homeland, deported to foreign lands, and their places filled by others dragged from different areas. The Northern Kingdom disappeared. The people were absorbed into the population of these foreign lands and never emerged again in history. All traces of what became of the people who were the Ten Tribes of Israel had vanished. The Northern Kingdom would never rise again.

About the turn of the sixth century B.C., a series of events began that within a few years would blot out Judah's place in the history of the ancient orient. The Chaldeans of Babylon under Nebuchadnezzar had conquered everything from the river Nile to the river Euphrates. In 598 B.C. Judah refused to pay tribute to Babylon and rebelled. The following year Nebuchadnezzar led his forces against Jehoiachin, the King of Judah. Nebuchadnezzar carried away all Jerusalem and Jehoiachin and his family were deported to Babylon.[1] Nebuchadnezzar allowed Judah to continue as a vassal-state. Jehoiachin was replaced on the throne by his uncle Mattaniah, who Nebuchadnezzar renamed Zedekiah.

Even though they saw the deportation of their families and knew of the bitter experiences of the Northern Kingdom, the Judaens still had the will to resist. Voices called out denouncing Babylon and demanding recovery for everything lost. When Zedekiah rebelled against the king of Babylon in 588 B.C., Nebuchadnezzar arrived with a strong army and with the speed of lightning, Judah fell before the divisions of infantry, calvary and charioteers.[2] The cities of Lachish, Azekah, and after a two year siege, the city of Jerusalem, all fell to Babylon. King Zedekiah was taken. His children were slaughtered before him and his eyes were put out.[3] Jerusalem was plundered, the royal palace and Temple were set on fire and the city walls and fortifications were razed to the ground.

In 587 B.C. once again part of the population was deported to Babylon. Nebuchadnezzar erased the royal House of David, which had reigned without interruption for 400 years. Judah became Babylon's province. A small group of guerrillas continued a conflict with the Babylonians. This resulted in a third deportation as reprisal. A few Judahites were able to escape into Egypt.[4] The Southern Kingdom became an empty land, the tribes of Israel were scattered. The end of the Kingdom of Judah marked the end of the history of ancient Israel. The history of the Jews now began.

Jeremiah from Jerusalem wrote to the elders, priests, prophets and to the whole nation under Nebuchadnezzar in Babylon: "Thus saith the Lord of hosts...Build you houses, and dwell in them; and plant gardens, and eat the fruit of them; take ye wives, and beget sons and daughters...that ye may be increased there, and not diminish. And seek peace of the city...for in peace there of shall ye have peace" (Jer. 29:4-7).

Following Jeremiah's well considered advice, the Jews did not fare badly. In fact, they fared very well. Nowhere were they forced into any heavy labor as had been the case in Egypt during the days of Moses. Babylon was a thriving economy. Never was so much building going on in the Mesopotamia as under Nebuchadnezzar. Trade and commerce were tremendous.

The children of Israel developed a new profession par excellence. They became merchants and traders. In their homeland they had been peasants, settlers, cattle breeders and tradesmen. The law of Israel had made no provision for commerce. "Canaanite" was synonymous with "shopkeeper" and "merchant," people who the prophets had castigated for their sins.[5]

The clever switch to commerce, added with their attachment to the faith of their fathers, proved to be the best guarantee of the continuance of Israel as a nation. As farmers and settlers they would have scattered throughout a foreign land and intermarried and interbred with people of other races. In a few generations the Jews would have been absorbed and disappeared, but this new profession required them to build houses and live in communities.[6] They devoted themselves to their religious practices, giving them unity and continuity.

An important institution came about during their exile — the rise of the synagogue. The pious Jews first gathered in houses on the Sabbath for prayer and the reading of their scriptures in place of the Temple sacrifices. The synagogue became so effective as a means of cementing the Jewish community together, providing an invaluable community center for religious instruction, that it has been a carefully maintained institution.

As an international trade center, Babylonia surpassed all other nations of the ancient orient. It was an ideal location for the Israelites to establish a new way of life. Industry and commerce were the great schools for cities and capitals over the whole world. Although the Jews had much to learn that would profit their future generations and raise their standard of living, they would never lose their heart yearnings for their homeland on the Jordan. They wouldn't forget the City of David, their beloved Jerusalem.

Approaching 500 B.C. the sun was setting on the ancient orient. The Assyrian Empire had reached its peak. It stretched from Upper Egypt to the Persian Gulf. From Egypt came one final attempt to keep from sinking into insignificance. The Pharaohs Necho and Apries made great efforts to reconquer Syria and Palestine. The new manifestations bore no fruit and success eluded their military exploits. The same thing happened on the Mediterranean. The power of the Phoenician merchant sailors began to decline. One century later, Greece had inherited their world trade.

Even Nebuchadnezzar was to be the last great ruler to sit on the throne of Babylon.[7] In the Babylonian School of Astronomy continuous observations were made of the heavens for 350 years, between 750 B.C. and 400 B.C. Undreamt advances allowed the priesthood to predict eclipses of the sun and the moon. Their astronomical accuracy even exceeded those of Europe until the 18th century. Architecture and literature flourished.

For 1,500 years the Fertile Crescent had been the oldest center of civilization since the Stone Age. The cosmic clock was moving on and history was leaving the great Semitic states like Egypt and Syria that had fulfilled their assignment. Man's early existence had helped prepare the way for the Indo-Germanic kingdoms which gave birth to Europe. Within a few centuries, new civilizations would appear, art would reach unimagined heights and the human mind in science and philosophy would soar to new pinnacles. It would bring from the ancient orient a practical system of weights and measurements, astronomy, writing, the alphabet and the Bible.[8]

22

5

Return to the Promised Land

Seven years after the death of Nebuchadnezzar in 555 B.C., Nabonidus ascended the throne of Babylon and thus became the last ruler from Mesopotamia. Iran was quickly heading for a great war. Led by Cyrus, the Persians overcame their neighbors, the Medes, who shared the Assyrian Empire with the Babylons. Astyages, the King of the Medes, was defeated by his grandson, Cyrus. Two years later Cyrus captured Ecbatana, the capital of the Kingdom of Media.

Babylonia, Lydia in Asia Minor, and Sparta formed an alliance against Cyrus. Croesus, the King of Lydia, attacked the Persians and was soundly defeated. This opened the way for Cyrus to invade Babylonia and Babylon. The Persians attacked Nabonidus in 539 B.C., and the Babylonian army was defeated. A year later, the King of Persia made his triumphal entry into Babylon. For the first time there were no columns of smoke rising, no shattered walls or houses plundered, no temples or palaces razed to the ground and no man was killed or imprisoned.

The Bible remembers Cyrus as an enlightened monarch. His unparalleled and swift rise to power was not marred by any recorded deed of violence. The tolerance he extended toward Babylon included religious practices. The images and shrines of the local gods were reerected. He did the same thing in the city of Ur.

Cyrus' tolerance was also extended to the Jews; after many years in exile, he would fulfill the Israelites' dearest wish. This meant permission for them to return to Jerusalem. A royal decree was issued in the form of a reparation. He regarded the Persians as successors of the Babylonians and ordered that all gold and silver which was taken from the Temple in Jerusalem be returned to Israel. Cyrus trusted Zerubbabel, a prince of Judah and probably a member of the House of David, to execute the order.

In 537 B.C., after 50 years of exile, not everyone would take advantage of this permission to leave the wealthy Babylon where the Jews had established themselves and return to Jerusalem. Most of the exiles remained in Babylon, with only a remnant returning to Palestine. After long preparation, a caravan of 42,000 set out on the 800 mile journey between Babylon and Jerusalem toward the old homeland.

Soon after its return, the foundations were laid for Zerubbabel's Temple. The rebuilding then advanced very slowly. The country was barren and conditions were extremely bleak. The people were wrapped in their own personal plight. It was not until 20 years after the foundation had been laid that the rebuilding of the Temple was taken up in earnest. Two prophets, Zechariah and Haggai, called the people to repent and work was undertaken with vigor. The efforts of the returned exiles were focused exclusively on the rebuilding for many years. Building began again in 520 B.C. and the Temple was completed in 515 B.C., 70 years following its destruction.[1]

The Jews made the Holy City the center of Jewry for all Jews — those who lived in the homeland of Judah and those who were scattered throughout the world. The high priest of the Temple in Jerusalem was head over all of Israel. Only a solid religious community could guarantee its existence in the face of unknown future political developments. It was abundantly clear that Israel's days of the Davidic monarchy were gone forever. Israel turned its back on politics and took no part in the affairs of the world during subsequent centuries.

24

The Persians were liege lords of Jerusalem for two centuries. During that time no violent variations seem to have taken place. In the 4th century B.C. the center of political power began to shift to the West. The Greeks had called a halt to further Persian advance during the previous century with two important battles. In 491 B.C. they defeated the Persian armies under Darius I and later defeated the Persian fleet in 480 B.C. Alexander the Great defeated Darius the III, king of Persia, in 333 B.C. Coins found show that Greek trade and influence had already penetrated everywhere in the orient long before the days of Alexander the Great.

The Macedonians rose to the leadership of the nations among the world. Their first target was Egypt. The infantry and cavalry marched down the coast of Syria and Palestine. Here they defeated the Phoenician city of Tyre[2] and the Philistine town of Gaza.[3] This then opened the road to the Nile. Alexander left the conquest of the inland territories to his general Parmenion. Jerusalem and the province of Judah submitted to their new masters peacefully. The Greek conqueror tolerated the way of life of the theocracy of Judah and left the religious community intact.

On the outermost tip of the Nile, the city of Alexandria was founded which became the new metropolis of the world. It became the center of intellectual life, attracting the best minds in the Greek and oriental worlds. Alexander guaranteed the Jews, who were the descendants of the refugees in the Babylonian era, the same rights as his own countrymen. This provision, carried on by his successors, led to Alexandria becoming a great reservoir of Jewish life and culture.

The spread of the Greek language throughout the Mediterranean basin and the encouragement that Alexander and his followers gave to Jewish colonization throughout the empire in time became the highways over which the Gospels would spread the Good News. Even before Alexander, the Greeks had reached out in a thousand different ways into Mesopotamia. But the Jews remained ignorant to the ways of the world and time stood still for the religious community that appears to have been influenced only by the Torah, the Law of God.

Greece was not a danger to the Jews from a growing ascendency, or militarism, or seductive temptations. The danger was the freer atmosphere of the modern world. Despite the new era of mankind, the theocracy held to past traditions. Eventually they would be forced to join issue with the new ideas. But there was still time enough before the second century B.C.

Alexander led one of the greatest and most successful military expeditions in history. Every country in the Ancient East fell before him. He pressed on to the Indus, to the foot of the Himalayas. On the way back, in 323 B.C., Alexander died from a fever at the age of 33. His generals had no scruples about getting rid of his family members by murdering them and dividing his empire into three kingdoms: the Kingdom of Macedonia in Northern Greece; the Kingdom of the Seleucids, which stretched from Thrace through Asia Minor and Syria to the border of India; and the Ptolemaic Kingdom which included Egypt and Judah.

Ptolemy I and his son Ptolemy II were the first rulers of the Ptolemaic Kingdom. They developed the capital city of Alexandria into a nursery of Hellenistic culture and learning. Its fame made it well known far beyond the borders of the kingdom and attracted emigrants from other nations, including those from Judah.

This crucible steeped itself in the beauty of the Greek language, which was then the language of international commerce and trading and the language of tens of thousands of Israelites who knew no other home. They could no longer follow the sacred Hebrew text in the services of the synagogue. Thus, by about 250 B.C., the Jews in Egypt decided to translate the Torah into the Greek language, an act of immeasurable importance for western civilization.

The legend of how the translation took place is based on Ptolemy II and his collection of the finest books in the world. He decided to add the five books of Moses — the greatest books of all — to his collection. He sent envoys to the high priest to ask for a copy of these books. At the same time he asked for men to be sent who could translate them into Greek. The high priest sent a copy of the Torah along with 72 learned and wise scribes.

On the island of Pharos, off the coast of Alexandria, they set out to translate the books, an extremely difficult task for which they had neither prototype nor dictionary. Each worked in a cell by himself. When the scholars had completed their work and all 72 translations were compared, they corresponded word for word. Accordingly, the Greek translation became known as the "Septuagint," which means "the Seventy." What had once been known only to a few, in the sanctuary, in the old tongue, and to one nation, was now available and intelligible for all people of other tongues and other nations.

Judah's attachment to the Kingdom of Ptolemies lasted for over 100 years, until 195 B.C. when the Seleucids of Antioch forced their way south into Palestine. The Seleucids defeated Potolemy V, and caused Palestine to once again come under a new sovereignty. Their attempts to compel the Jews to adopt Greek polytheism reached its most agonizing heights during the reign of Antiochus IV. The prophet Daniel epitomized him as to what the Antichrist shall be. His vicious assault on Judea was an indication of the barbarity of his nature.

Greek customs and philosophy were imposed as a part of Syrian policy for Palestine. The Greek attitude and influence became more apparent than at any time since it had began to infiltrate during Alexander's campaigns. Gradually, and for the first time, the foreign seed began to sprout even in the theocracy. Onias III, the Zadokite high priest, led the resistance against Hellenistic infiltration. According to the Book I Maccabees, in 175 B.C. Onias, the last genuine high priest, had his office stolen from him by his brother Jason who used underhanded means to become the high priest and brought his nation into Greekish fashion. The priesthood in Jerusalem then took an important part in the encouragement of the Hellenization of the land. Greek influence grew to its height and an increase in heathenish manners prevailed.

Jason and his priests did not serve at the altar, despised the Temple and neglected the sacrifices. Instead, they became partakers of the unlawful game of discus in the place of exercise. Why would Yahweh be so displeased with it, and how could the high priest be denounced as ungodly? The place of exercise was the stadium. Jason built the stadium under the Temple's tower. The orthodox Jews must have been greatly terrified to come face to face with Greece just a few steps from the sanctuary of Temple, the Holy of Holies.

The playing of Olympic games in those days required that they be played completely naked. The body could only be covered with a thin coat of oil. When the Jewish athletes appeared in contests away from home, they were met with ridicule and sarcasm. It was not long before they were guilty of the serious crime of becoming uncircumcised. They used a surgical operation to restore their natural state.[4]

But there was another, deeper significance attached to the performance of athletics. It was a religious exercise dedicated to the gods Apollo and Zeus. Invocations to these pagan deities opened the games — on this, the orthodox Jews could not be compromised. Foremost in the conservative reaction against the temporizing policies of the Jerusalem priests was a religious group called the Hasidim, which means the "pious ones."[5] The Hasidim alone strongly opposed the infiltration of Greek culture.

Antiochus launched an attack against Egypt, his archenemy. Frustrated after his defeat, he vented his anger on the city of Jerusalem as his soldiers marched through Judea on the way homeward. King Antiochus gained possession of the city through trickery. He plundered and desecrated the Temple in Jerusalem. On Dec. 25, 168 B.C., he offered Zeus a sow on the altar, an act of sacrilege and blasphemy referred to by Daniel as an "abomination of desolation."

Plundering temples was Antiochus' specialty.[6] However the treasures of the Temple were not enough for him. The Seleucid king sent his tax collector Apollonius with an armed force to Jerusalem. When he had taken the spoils of the city, he set it on fire and pulled down the walls on every side of the city in an outpouring of rage. He had 40,000 Jews slaughtered and another 40,000 carried into slavery.

Israel had suffered through almost every horror and ignominy imaginable but neither under the Assyrians nor under the Babylonians did they receive such a blow as the edict issued by Antiochus IV, called Epiphanes to destroy the faith of Israel.[7] Antiochus' objective was to convert or kill. For taking any part in any Jewish religious ceremony, the traditional sacrifices, the Sabbath, circumcision or for possessing any of the Hebrew scriptures, the penalty was death. These decrees were enforced with unbelievable ferocity. The Holy Scriptures were destroyed. Thousands of manuscripts which had taken hundreds of thousands of hours to transcribe were burned. The worship of Zeus was set up in the Temple of Yahweh. Pagan alters were erected in cities and towns throughout Judea. It was the first total religious persecution in history. A reign of terror had descended over the troubled land.

Severe laws were particularly directed at the Hasidim. At first the Hasidim suffered passively. They were massacred, without offering resistance, rather than break the Sabbath when attacked by the pro-Greek faction.[8] Many of them, "zealous for righteousness and the Law," flocked into the desert to "the Land of Damascus" to avoid defilement.[9] The community settled into the area under domination of the Nabataean kings who also ruled over Damascus. In their new land of refuge they lived in the natural caves in the hills overlooking the Dead Sea. They removed their valuable manuscripts to the caves to protect the word of Yahweh from being destroyed under the new laws.

6

The Hasmonean Dynasty

In a small village, just 20 miles outside of Jerusalem in the highlands of Judah, lived the priest Mattathias with his five sons. When Antiochus' officers came to Modin to force the inhabitants to forsake the Law, Mattathias killed the king's commissioner.[1] This act was the signal for open resistance, a life and death struggle for religious freedom — The War of the Maccabees.

Mattathias and his sons rallied their followers and waged fierce guerrilla warfare from their mountain stronghold against the occupying Seleucids. After the death of Mattathias, his son Judas, whose surname Maccabeus meant "the Hammer," became the leader. In the highlands of Judah, the band achieved their first success. The small group of rebels completely mastered the numerically superior, well drilled occupation troops. They captured Beth-Haron, Emmous and Beth Zur. The Seleucids were forced to retreat until reinforcements arrived from Antioch.

Judas Maccabaeus liberated Jerusalem in 164 B.C. and restored the old Order of the Temple. The altar was restored and sacrifices were offered to Yahweh as in former times.[2] His good fortunes continued over Judah, Galilee, Transjordan, and wherever Israelites remained true to the old faith.

King Antiochus Epiphanes was compelled to send his son Antiochus V, known as Eupator, with a large force to intervene. The Seleucids marched a massive army with elephants, flanked by detachments of calvary. The Maccabeans were unable to cope with so much force and were defeated. Surprisingly, the victors made peace with very favorable terms. The decrees of Antiochus IV Epiphanes during 167 B.C. were rescinded, religious freedom was granted, and the religious community was once more recognized. The Jewish rebellion had achieved its aims.

In 162 B.C., Alcimus was promoted to high priest. The Hasidim were prepared to recognize this "Son of Aaron" as the high priest but, for reasons unknown, their trust was deceived and he put 60 of them to death. Compromised with the Maccabees and betrayed by Alcimus, the Hasidim returned to the desert to "grope their way" until a new leader, the priestly Teacher of Righteousness, appeared to lead them.[3]

A new struggle for political freedom was begun by Judas Maccabaeus' brothers, Jonathan and Simon. Syrian military intervention in Judah ended in 159 B.C. The Pontifical throne became unoccupied when Alcimus died from a stroke in that same year. In 152 B.C. Jonathan was promoted to be high priest by Alexander Balas, the new Selencid king. Jonathan took the office although he was neither of pontifical descent nor had any real interest in religious matters. Jonathan then governed the nation and continued to cleanse the country of Hellenism.

The Hasidim constituted the main priestly element firmly attached to the Zadokite pontifical dynasty which held supreme power in the Temple of Jerusalem from the time of Solomon for 400 years. They believed that the line of Zadok should be returned to the throne. Jonathan betrayed God for the sake of riches amassed by plundering the Hellenophile Jews and neighboring Gentiles. The Teacher of Righteousness and his followers viewed Jonathan's claims to high priest as worthless, his behavior objectionable. They referred to Jonathan as: "the 'Wicked Priest,' who was called by the name of truth, a true disciple of Moses, before he assumed the office of High Priest."[4]

Jonathan was captured by the Selucid king in 143 B.C. and put to death. This marked the return of a group of the Hasidim to Jerusalem. These priests took with them those scribes who were loyal to them and they separated from the rest of the community left behind in the wilderness.[5] They became known as the Pharisees ("Pharisee" means "separated"). To the priesthood left behind, the death of the Wicked Priest did not mark the end of the domination of Israel by other illegitimate priests who continued to lead the nation astray.[6] These outlaw priests incurred the same guilt as the Wicked Priest. They amassed their wealth by plundering the common people. They taught false doctrine, adopted the Gentile calender and they were condemned by the community for their cruelty.

Simon, the brother of Judas Maccabaeus, replaced Jonathan and this established the beginning of the Maccabean or Hasmonean Dynasty. The struggle with Syria ended when Judah was granted political freedom, and a new group of priests came into power. The Sadducees were swept into power by their support of the Hasmonean priest-generals and were already in control when independence finally came.

The name "Sadducee" is probably derived from Zadok. Sadducee implies a claim of descent from the first to hold the sacred office; this also implied legitimacy. The Sadducees' power was centralized in Jerusalem through their control of the Temple. They were not a large party, including only the Jerusalem hierarchy, aristocrats, and the majority of farmers and landowners. Under the Hasmonean princes of this later period who learned from previous mistakes, the pro-Hellenizing policies were administered more adroitly than during the times of Antiochus Epiphanes.

Sadducees were great political compromisers. They led sophisticated lives, were educated and wealthy. The Sadducees were the apex of Jewish aristocracy and had virtually no following among the masses. They accepted no revelation beyond the five books of Moses. They rejected ideas such as immortality, resurrection, angels and demons. Theirs was a rational religion preoccupied more with matters of current expedient interest than eternal truths, even to the point of compromising with Greek and Roman paganism.

The Pharisees maintained beliefs close to those who remained behind in the desert. The Pharisees believed in immortality, heaven and hell, and a general resurrection. They also believed that the free will was limited by the predestined purposes of God. They held that the practices of the Sadducees were inconsistent with the obligations of high priesthood.

The Pharisees were proselytizers, believing in an international Jewish community. One might enter the church if he accepted the Jewish Law and the Pharisaic ritual requirements that were administered through the synagogues. They took a deeply ethical view of religion. The only political issue they cared about was religious freedom. They repudiated apocalyptic messianism and adhered strictly to the text of the Bible and its approved interpretations.[7] The Pharisees believed in moderation in all things.

Simon was murdered in 134 B.C. by a son-in-law of Ptolemy and the political and spiritual leadership along with the office of high priest was transferred to John Hyrcanus in accordance with the designation of the people under Simon's rule. Under his rule, John Hyrcanus undertook military campaigns to expand his sphere of power. His military campaigns were successful but he received little acclaim from the masses. He was openly opposed by the Pharisees who were concerned with shaping their lives according to the Law of God and disapproved of the Hasmonean's drive for worldly power.

A Pharisee named Eleazar called for Hyrcanus to relinquish his position of high priest, because during the time of Antiochus Epiphanes, Hyrcanus' mother had been in prison. Due to the possibility that a woman may have been violated while in prison, the son of such a mother was not fit to rule as high priest. This angered Hyrcanus, and he regarded it as the opinion held by all of the Pharisees. In fact, they did not view him as satisfying the prescription of the Law concerning the purity of high priests. Hyrcanus persecuted the Pharisees and many of them fled back to the community in the desert.[8]

After the death of Hyrcanus, his son Aristobulus became high priest. Aristobulus became the first Jewish ruler to secure the title of king. He continued the military campaigns and forced his conquered territories to practice circumcision. Forced conversion did not further religious aims but subjugated more people to the power of the king. Aristobulus died after only one year in office.

Aristobulus' wife handed the throne to his brother Jonathan. She then became his wife. Jonathan Grecized his name to Jannaeus and called himself Alexander Jannaeus. Alexander Jannaeus waged many wars and, like his predecessors, he was also successful. Under his leadership, the area occupied almost covered the territories once occupied by the kingdoms of Israel and Judah.

The Pharisees stood in open opposition to the policy of the ruler. Even as a man of war they believed he simultaneously had to fill the post of high priest. He did not shrink from suppressing the Pharisees or enforcing his will on them with cruelty and ruthlessness. The Pharisees encouraged the Seleucid king, Demetrius III, to invade Judah. But when he was unable to capitalize on his initial victory and he returned to Syria, Jannaeus had 800 Pharisees put to death.

Jannaeus evoked horror among the people with a cruel punishment they had never seen before. Alexander Jannaeus had the Pharisees executed by hanging them alive on trees. He arranged a banquet for his women in front of the crosses and had the wives and children of the Pharisees slain "before the eyes of the crucified men."[9] Jannaeus destroyed open resistance, but the inward rejection of the populace continued.

From John Hyrcanus to Aristobulus II, the policy of the Hasmonean rulers was one of conquest and plunder at the expense of their neighbors. Over time, the Seleucids became a diminishing threat. Rome overthrew Hannibal of Carthage and was expanding its sovereignty beyond Greece into Asia

Minor. Pompey, the Roman general, marched through the Kingdom of the Seleucids into Palestine.

Various factions in Judea sent delegations to Damascus to negotiate for Roman favor. John Hyrcanus II, lineal descendant of Maccabees and high priest, was given the nod by Pompey. He surrendered Jerusalem to the Romans in return for political favors. Although he was stripped of the title of king, he was appointed ethnarch of Judea. In 63 B.C. the Roman legions entered Jerusalem and Judah became a province of Rome. The short political independence of Israel came to an abrupt end.

7

Life Under the Romans

The Roman Empire extended from North Africa and Spain to the shores of Asia Minor. The will of Rome reigned supreme. After the disappearance of the great Semetic Empires of the Fertile Crescent, Palestine was drawn into the new world and shared its destiny. Roman roads connected every city in the empire. The trade routes and commerce, along with good communications, were enhanced by a common language. Rome enforced its will through occupation troops and appointed nominees who ruled and exploited the land. Life in the Roman Empire was largely Greek civilization.

Anyone wandering through Palestine at the turn of the eras might have imagined he was in Greece. Greek was the universal language which united all people of the east. Greek dress and a Greek way of life had long penetrated into the purely Jewish communities. Judeans wore the same clothes as those worn in Athens, Rome and Alexandria. These included a tunic and cloak, shoes or sandals, and a hat as head covering. Across the Jordan lay the Decapolis. The Ten Cities of the Gospels took Athens as their model.[1] They had temples which were sacred to Zeus and Artemis. They had their theatre, pillared forum, stadium, gymnasium and baths. Caesarea, the seat of Pilate's government which lay just south of Carmel, was steeped in Greek architecture, as well as the Greek way of life. So, too, were Sepphoris, Tiberias, Caseara Philippi and Jericho. Only the small towns and villages in Galilee and in Judah retained their Jewish style of architecture. It was in these small towns of genuine Jewish communities that Jesus later lived and taught.

The Romans allowed the Jews to have their own rulers for the first few years. Then in 37 B.C. the limited autonomy they had enjoyed was choked off by the imposition of a man who Rome chose to lead the Jews, Herod the Great. Herod was brutal but the Romans recognized him as an able administrator. After his appointment, it took him three years to subjugate the population. Twelve more years were spent in consolidating his hold on the throne.

The persistent threat to Herod's authority was the Hasmonean spirit. The Sadducees, with their political ambitions, were most closely aligned with the Hasmoneans. Out of necessity, Herod aligned himself with the Pharisees. One of his first acts was to slaughter 45 leading Sadducee leaders in Jerusalem. He promoted Pharisees in their stead for they were not interested in politics and did not pose a threat. The Sadducees did not recover their earlier supremacy until after the death of Herod.[2]

Herod was more Roman than Jewish. It was his desire to weld Roman paganism to Judaism. He totally disregarded the hereditary office of high priest, appointing and removing men at will. He spent lavishly on pagan temples. One by one, he had the remaining Hasmonean family murdered, including his Hasmonean wife, Marianne, the woman who he really loved. By 25 B.C. the last heirs-apparent of the Hasmonean family had been disposed of and Herod's crown was finally secure.

Herod's kingdom included not only Jews, but Gentiles as well. He did not continue the Hasmonean policy of converting Gentiles to Judaism by force, but instead placed Jews and Gentiles side-by-side with equal rights. He wanted to be a Jew to the Jews and a Greek to the Greeks.

The next years of Herod's life were his greatest achievement. His most significant contribution was in the area of building. He surrounded himself with educated Hellenists and furthered the building activities in the Greek cities. In spite of the introduction of Roman baths, gymnasia, race tracks, theaters, temples and other features of pagan life, Herod the diplomat tried to win Jewish favor by rebuilding the Temple in Jerusalem.

Herod's Temple was to be his crowning glory. Zerubbabel's Temple never had the glory or grandeur of Solomon's. Herod followed the basic example of the earlier Temple but on a scale even grander than Solomon's. One thousand priests were trained as artisans. Material and workmen were assembled. Huge blocks of white marble adorned with gold were brought to the city. The work began in 20 B.C. and although most of the Temple was complete before the death of Herod,[3] its final completion came just two years before it was destroyed in A.D. 70.

Prior to his death, Herod sought to determine the succession to his throne. His kingdom was divided among his three sons: Archelaus, Herod Antipas and Philip. Archelaus became ruler over Judea, Samaria and Idumea. Antipas received Galilee and Perea, which lay east of the Jordan. Philip was to reign over the region east of the Jordan in the northern part of the kingdom. This disposition had to be confirmed by Rome to become legally effective. Antipas and Philip were named tetrarchs and Archelaus received the title of ethnarch. To the people, the distinctions in title meant nothing and to them, the rulers were the same as kings.[4]

Archelaus was the most hated of the three monarchs because he ruled so brutally and arbitrarily.[5] The subjects of Archelaus sent an embassy to Augustus in Rome and gained a hearing. In A.D. 6 Archelaus was exiled to Gaul. His territory was placed under a Roman governor, Quirinius, who ordered a general census of the people in Syria and Palestine. This was 13 years after the census that required Mary and Joseph to go to the native home of Joseph to be enrolled.

During the time of Jesus, Galilee and the northern part of

the land east of Jordan were under the rule of Jewish princes. Samaria, Judea and Idumea were ruled by the Roman governor, Pontius Pilate.[6] Pilate's office was marked by corruption, violence, depravation, illegal executions, ill treatment, and incessant, unbearable cruelty. His conduct was so hard and ruthless, he was finally recalled to Rome to account for his actions.

The Zealots were founded by Judas the Galilean. He led a revolt against Rome for establishing a census for the purpose of collecting taxes. The Zealots opposed the payment of tribute by Israel to a foreign power, particularly to a pagan emperor. They believed this to be treason to God and sought to follow the same footsteps as Mattathias and the Maccabee heroes who resisted the Seleucid Empire and its attempt to paganize their land.

The Romans quickly wiped out Judas and his followers along with their revolt. However, their zeal for the Law and for their nation was not crushed by the Romans. Members of Judas' family continued as Zealot leaders. Two of his sons were crucified in A.D. 46. A third son, Menahem, attempted to seize control in the revolution against Rome in A.D. 66. It is likely that this Zealot agitation did much to ferment the outbreak of the disastrous war which ended in the destruction of the Jewish nation in A.D. 70.

After the war, the Sadducees disappeared with the destruction of the Temple. The Pharisees, who had concentrated their power in the synagogues, survived and flourished. This provided the basis for rabbinical tradition forming what is today modern orthodox Judaism. The Zealots fought the Romans until A.D. 73 when the last of their band was defeated at the fortress of Masada, not far from the Dead Sea. There the last 960 held out against a lengthy Roman siege. Rather than be taken prisoners by the Roman army, they committed mass suicide.

8

The Community of Qumran

"And when these become members of the Community in Israel according to all these rules, they shall separate from the habitation of ungodly men and shall go into the wilderness to prepare the way of Him; as it is written, 'Prepare in the wilderness the way of the Lord. Make straight in the desert a path for our God.' This path is the study of the Law which He commanded by the hand of Moses, that they may do according to all that has been revealed from age to age, and as the Prophets have revealed by His Holy Spirit" (The Community Rule VIII:12-16).

A group of religious patriots went into the Judaen desert in 167 B.C. They believed they were the "Remnant of Israel" chosen by God to prepare in the wilderness "the way of the Lord." This group of the Hasidim that fled into the desert was eschatologically oriented — that is, they were concerned with the End of Times.[1] They sincerely believed that time was running out. They called the "Sons of Darkness" those who were under the demonic power of Belial and destined for destruction. The final battle was drawing near, one which would pit the chosen ones, the "Sons of Light," against the "Sons of Darkness." It would be truth against falsehood, right against wrong.

41

The chosen ones went into the wilderness to fulfill the Scriptures, to avoid contamination and to retain their purity by living their lives according to God's commands, as if they were already in the new age. There on the desert plateau overlooking the Dead Sea, they led austere, disciplined and dedicated lives. They lived on the marl terrace, reading, copying and meditating upon the scriptures. Religious meditations, sacred meals and assemblies made up their daily routine. It would seem that from the standpoint of man's ethical perspective, God might look on the men at Qumran with utmost favor. They alone held the key to the whole process. They alone had kept the ancient covenant.

The men of Qumran called themselves the "Covenant" *(berith)*, and specifically the "New Covenant" *(berith hadashah)*. Other names were the "Congregation" *('edah)*, "Assembly" *(qahal)*, "Party" *('esah,* sometimes also meaning "Council"), and "Community" *(yahad)*, a word conveying the idea of "unity," and these last two are often combined into "Party of the Community" *('esath ha-yahad)*. This idea of unity lay very close to the heart of the Community, and the same word *yahad* is used often adverbially meaning "in common." Thus they shared all the necessities of life — spiritual, as well as material.[2]

Accounts given by three historians give a clearer picture of the Community's way of life. Writings by Pliny the Elder, Philo Judaeus and Flavius Josepheus, along with the Community's own writings, provide the evidence to piece together the information to give a complete understanding of the Brotherhood and its way of life.

Pliny the Elder was an educated Roman who served Titus in the Jewish War of A.D. 66-70. He was a diligent and accurate writer. In Book V of his voluminous work *Naturalis Historia*, he describes the Essenes as living on the west side of the Dead Sea, set back from the shore. They were a solitary race, and strangely above all others in the entire world. They lived without women and renounced sexual love. They shunned money and lived among the palm trees. Day by day their numbers were renewed by those who flocked to them from afar, wearied of battling with life's daily troubles. Engedi lied to the south of them.

Philo Judaeus lived in Alexandria during the time of Christ. He was not only a Hellenistic scholar but also a strictly observant Jew. His strength of religious loyalty is indicative of the Jew's sense of identity in the communities of the Dispersion. Philo is most noted for his work *Divine Reason*, and his leadership of the Jewish embassy to Rome to persuade Caligula not to set up a statue of himself in the Holy of Holies. He has written describing the Essaei:

"Worshipers of God, they yet did not sacrifice animals, regarding a reverent mind as the only true sacrifice. At first they lived in villages and avoided cities, in order to escape the contagion of evils rife therein. They pursued agriculture and other peaceful arts, but accumulated no gold or silver. Least of all were any slaves found among them, for they saw in slavery a violation of the law of nature, which made all men free brethren...

"Natural philosophy they only studied as far as it teaches that there is a God who made and watches over all things. Moral philosophy was their chief preoccupation; their conduct was regulated by their national Jewish laws. They especially studied these laws on the seventh day, which they held holy, leaving off all work upon it...

"In their synagogues they sat down in ranks, the older ones above the younger. Then one took and read the Bible, while the rest listened attentively, and another who was very learned would expound whatever was obscure in the lesson...

"No one had his private house, but shared his dwelling with all; and living as they did in colonies they threw open their doors to any of their sect who came their way. They had a common storehouse, common expenditures, common clothing, common food eaten in common meals. This was made possible by putting whatever they earned each day into a common fund, which supported the sick when they could not work. Their old people were objects of reverence and honor and were treated by the rest as parents are by real children."

Flavius Josephus was the Jewish historian who wrote his account of the Essenes in *The Jewish Antiquities*. He tried to persuade his countrymen not to resist the Roman armies under Vespasian but joined with them in the war against Rome. He was later shrewd enough when captured to prophesy that Vespasian was fated to become emperor, and thus was granted a pardon by Rome.

"These Essens reject pleasures as an evil, but esteem continence, and the conquest over our passions, to be virtue. They neglect wedlock, but choose out other person's children, while they are pliable, and fit for learning; and esteem them to be of their kindred, and form them according to their own manners. They do not absolutely deny the fitness of marriage, and the succession of mankind thereby continued; but they guard against the lascivious behavior of women, and are persuaded that none of them preserve their fidelity to one man.

"These men are despisers of riches, and so very communicative as raises our admiration. Nor is there any one to be found among them who hath more than another; for it is law among them, that those who come to them must let what they have be common to the whole order...

"They have no certain city, but many of them dwell in every city; and if any of their sect come from other places, what they have lies open for them, just as if it were their own...

"And as for their piety towards God, it is very extraordinary; for before sun-rising they speak not a word about profane matters, but put up certain prayers which they received from their forefathers, as if they made a supplication for its rising. After this, every one of them are sent away by their curators, to exercise some of those arts wherein they are skilled, in which they labor with great diligence till the fifth hour. After which they assemble themselves together again into one place; and when they have clothed themselves in white veils, they then bathe their bodies in cold water. And after this purification is over, they everyone meet together in an apartment of their own, into which it is not permitted to any other sect to enter; while they go, after a pure manner, into the dining room, as into a certain holy temple, and quietly set themselves down; upon which the baker lays them loaves in order; the cook also brings a single plate of one sort of food, and sets it before everyone of them; but a priest says grace before meat; and it is unlawful for any one to taste of the food before grace be said.

"They are eminent for fidelity, and are the ministers of peace; whatsoever they say is firmer than an oath; but swearing is avoided by them, and they esteem it worse than perjury; for they say, that he who cannot be believed without swearing by God is already condemned...

"But now, if any one hath a mind to come over to their sect, he is not immediately admitted, but he is prescribed the same method of living which they use, for a year, while he continues excluded; and they give him a small hatchet, and the forementioned girdle, and the white garment. And when he hath given evidence, during that time, that he can observe their continence, he approaches nearer to their way of living, and is made a partaker of the waters of purification; yet is not even now admitted to live with them; for after this demonstration of his fortitude, his temper is tried two more years, and if he appears to be worthy, they then admit him into their society. And before he is allowed to touch their common food, he is obliged to take tremendous oaths; that, in the first place, he will exercise piety towards God; and then, that he will observe justice towards men...and that he will neither conceal anything from those of his own sect, nor discover any of their doctrines to others, no, not though anyone should compel him so to do at the hazard of his life...

"What they most honor, after God himself, is the name of their legislator Moses, whom if anyone blaspheme, he is punished capitally. They also think it a good thing to obey their elders, and no one of them will speak while the other nine are against it...Moreover, they are stricter than any other of the Jews in resting from their labors on the seventh day; for they not only get their food ready the day before, that they may not be obliged to kindle a fire on that day, but they will not move any vessel out of its place...

"Now after the time of their preparatory trial is over, they are parted into four classes; and so far are the juniors inferior to the seniors, that if the seniors should be touched by the juniors, they must wash themselves, as if they had intermixed themselves with the company of a foreigner. They are long-lived also; insomuch that many of them live above a hundred years, by means of the simplicity of their diet; nay, as I think, by means of the regular course of life they observe also. They condemn the miseries of life, and are above pain, by the generosity of their mind.

"There are also those among them who undertake to foretell things to come, by reading the holy books, and using several sorts of purifications, and being perpetually conversant in the discourses of the prophets; and it is but seldom that they miss in their predictions.

"Moreover, there is another order of Essens, who agree with the rest as to their way of living, and customs, and laws, but differ from them in the point of marriage, as thinking that by not marrying they cut off the principal part of human life, which is the prospect of succession; nay rather, that if all men should be of the same opinion, the whole race of mankind would fail."

These accounts may not be entirely consistent but they clearly describe Qumran and the Community that lived there. It must be remembered that there were many Essene communities, some were small Jewish towns, and some were located in camps. Their number, by the estimation of Josephus, totaled 4,000. The members of the monastery were the priests and scribes of the Essenes and they lived by more stringent rules than their congregation.

Based on the size of the monastery at Qumran, the total number of monks who lived there during the time of Jesus probably totaled less than 40. A great number was not required to direct the religious rites and observe the holy days according to the Law. In their own writings they required a minimum number of participants for their holy banquets and the coming of the Messiah at the Triumphal Banquet.[3]

For those members in the Community who lived in urban areas outside of Qumran, their daily life was subject to somewhat less rigorous rules but their hopes and ideas were identical to their desert brethren. They kept the faith alive not only throughout Judea but also in the Diaspora.[4] Some of the scraps of manuscripts found in the Qumran caves written in Greek indicate that the Community had active communication with followers outside of Judea, such as in Syria and Egypt where Greek was the common language.[5] It was the Essenes of the Diaspora that had an impact on Paul when he developed his themes for the early Christian church. They were convinced that their beliefs and way of life conformed to the will of God and qualified them as being the only True Israel.

Each small town and camp was entrusted with its own lay leaders to direct the religious rites throughout the Community. These men not only performed their regular daily tasks but were also the religious leaders for their groups. The final reward for obeying the Law of Moses and leading a life according to the New Covenant was to be laid in the cemetery where one day the Messiah would come and raise His faithful back to life.

The Essenes located their monastery at the foot of the Vale of Achor which is today's modern Buqei'a, or "Little Plain," a five-mile plateau running above and parallel with the cliffs of Qumran. Hosea speaks of the Vale as a "Gate of Hope:" "Therefore, behold, I will allure her [the house of Judah], and bring her into the wilderness, and speak tenderly to her. And there I will give her her vineyards, and make the Valley of Achor a Gate of Hope. And there she shall answer as in the days of her youth, as at the time when she came out of the land of Egypt" (Hosea 2:14-15).

The Hosea passage serves as a proof text for the Essene exile and regeneration.[6] The Essenes believed the Sons of Light would assemble at the Gate and return from the desert to Jerusalem at the End of Days to wage war against evil. The religious and eschatological significance of the Vale of Achor was not lost upon the Essenes.

The Community occupied Qumran from 167 B.C. until the Jewish War with Rome. During the time of Herod, the influence and power of the Pharisees expanded, as did that of the Essenes when the Hasmonean dynasty was put to its end. An earthquake in 31 B.C. damaged part of the monastery, leaving its mark right across the settlement.[7] To the Essenes, who took this to be a sign from God, it meant that they were to leave Qumran and return to Jerusalem.

Herod was favorably disposed to the Essenes. One of the Essene priests named Menahem prophesied a royal and prosperous destiny for him. Philo wrote, "Menahem the Essene had foretold young Herod that someday he would be king and he esteemed the Essenes greatly." Menahem did well for himself and for the Essenes as well.[8] Josephus records that Herod always treated the Essenes with honor.

The priests located in Jerusalem in what is now known as the Essene Quarter in Jerusalem on Mt. Zion.[9] The priesthood never numbered more than in the desert though many more Essene pilgrims visited there and stayed in the nearby marl caves. The Essene Gate is identified by Josephus in The Jewish War (V, 145) as along the First Wall near the area of the Bethso with arrangements for mikvehs or cisterns for ritual baths even as at Qumran.[10] It was on Mt. Zion in the Essene Quarter that Jesus with his disciples celebrated the Last Supper and it is believed that here he appeared to them three days later. No other topographic location of the early Christian church has had so persistent and thorough a documentation as the Upper Room, where the first group of 120 followers used to gather.

Political conflict and unrest upon Herod's death caused the Community to return to Qumran after leaving approximately 30 years before. The emigration took place and once again the monastery at Qumran was occupied. They rebuilt their walls and wrote their commentaries. The Community flourished through the ministries of both Jesus and John the Baptist.

9

The Scrolls of the Community

To understand the Community at Qumran, it is necessary to study their literary works to see them as they saw themselves. To their contemporaries of the divided Macedonian Empire and later in the vast Roman Empire, they were a small, insignificant Jewish sect.[1] They had no power or influence and constituted no possible importance in history. This was not the view they took of themselves. They believed they were chosen to play the leading role in events that would change history so profoundly that the existing world order would be brought to an end and the new order would begin.

Over 700 manuscripts have come from the caves in Qumran. The scrolls contain copies of all the extant Hebrew Canon, except Esther. The best preserved texts are the books of Samuel and Numbers, along with archaic copies of Samuel and Jeremiah that date back earlier than 200 B.C. There is a second century B.C. copy of Daniel which must be no later than 50 years after the composition of the book itself. The most popular reading at Qumran appears to have been Deuteronomy — 14 copies found, and Isaiah — 12 copies found. There are 10 copies of the Psalms and eight of the minor prophets. There is a large number of Apocryphal[2] and Pseudepigraphal[3] works, most of the Damascus Document, and a large number of biblical commentaries, such as the Commentary on Nahum.

Their apocalyptic writings develop descriptions of a future age in elaborate terms clothed in a visionary language. The basic pattern of these writings is comprised of five elements: 1) The Coming of the Messiah, 2) The Work of the Messiah, 3) The Resurrection of the Dead, 4) The Day of Atonement – The Final Judgment and 5) The Glorious Age of the Kingdom of God. The most important of these writings are: 1) The Manual of Discipline, 2) The Damascus Document, 3) The War Between the Sons of Light and the Sons of Darkness, 4) The Thanksgiving Hymns and 5) The Messianic Rule. These are the heart of what is known as the Dead Sea Scrolls. From these is derived most of the information for our knowledge of the Qumran Community, its ideals and its practices.

The following excerpts are taken from the translation of the scrolls by G. Vermes in his book *The Dead Sea Scrolls in English*. It is one of the best translations, easy to read, and most readily accessible.

THE MANUAL OF DISCIPLINE

The Manual of Discipline forms the rules by which the Community lived. It is probably the oldest document of the priesthood, dating back to the second century B.C.[4] The Community believed that if they were removed from contact with the outside world they would obtain a clearer view of God. The translation is by G. Vermes.

A. Entry into the Covenant

The code to enter the covenant is very strict. One must seek God and do what He has commanded through the hand of Moses. One must love all that is good and hate all that is evil. One must pledge knowledge, powers and possessions to the Community of God. The importance of observing the correct calendar in observing religious holidays is also emphasized.

"The Master shall teach the saints to live according to the

50

Book of the Community Rule, that they may seek God with a whole heart and soul, and do what is good and right before Him as He commanded by the hand of Moses and all His servants the Prophets; that they may love all that He has chosen and hate all that He has rejected; and that they may love all the sons of light, each according to his lot in God's design, and hate all the sons of darkness, each according to his guilt in God's vengeance.

"All those who freely devote themselves to His truth shall bring all their knowledge, powers, and possessions into the Community of God, that they may purify their knowledge in the truth of God's precepts and order their powers according to His ways of perfection and all their possessions according to His righteous counsel. They shall not depart from any command of God concerning their times; they shall be neither early nor late for any of their appointed times; they shall stray neither to right nor to left of any of His true precepts. All those who embrace the Community Rule shall enter into the Covenant before God to obey all His Commandments so that they may not abandon Him during the dominion of Satan because of fear or terror or affliction.

"And the Priests shall bless all the men of the lot of God who walk perfectly in all His ways, saying: 'May He bless you with all good and preserve you from all evil! May He lighten your heart with life-giving wisdom and grant you eternal knowledge! May He raise His merciful face towards you for everlasting bliss!'

"And the Levites[5] shall curse all the men of the lot of Satan, saying: 'Be cursed because of all your guilty wickedness! May He deliver you up for torture at the hands of the vengeful Avengers! May He visit you with destruction by the hand of all the Wreakers of Revenge! Be cursed without mercy because of the darkness of your deeds! Be damned in the shadowy place of everlasting fire! May God not heed when you call Him, nor pardon you by blotting out your sin! May He raise His angry face towards you for vengeance! May there be no "Peace" for you in the mouth of those who hold fast to the

Fathers!' And after the blessing and the cursing all those entering the Covenant shall say, 'Amen, Amen.' "

B. Statues of the Council

The Community was hierarchical. Each man in Israel may be made aware of his status in God's community. An annual review of each individual was made in an effort to determine if he was to be upgraded or downgraded.

"Thus shall they do, year by year, for as long as the dominion of Satan endures. The Priests shall enter first, ranked one after another according to the perfection of their spirit; then the Levites; and thirdly, all the people one after another, in their Thousands, Hundreds, Fifties, and Tens, that every Israelite may know his place in the Community of God according to the everlasting design. No man shall move down from his place nor move up from his allotted position.

"No man shall be in the Community of His truth who refuses to enter the Covenant of God so that he may walk in the stubbornness of his heart, for his soul detests the wise teaching of just laws. He shall not be counted among the upright for he has not persisted in the conversion of his life.

"He shall neither be purified by atonement, nor cleansed by purifying waters, nor sanctified by seas and rivers, nor washed clean with any ablution. Unclean, unclean shall he be. For as long as he despises the precepts of God he shall receive no instruction in the Community of His counsel.

"For it is through the spirit of the true counsel concerning the ways of man that all his sins shall be expiated that he may contemplate the light of holiness uniting him to His truth, and his iniquity shall be expiated by the spirit of uprightness and humility."

C. The Master's Hymn

This section is intended for the instructor who brings others to the inner vision. There is so strong a resemblance in this part of the scroll to the writings of the Gospel according to

St. John and to the Epistles of St. John that many believe St. John was influenced by this passage.

"The Master shall instruct all the sons of light and shall teach them the nature of all the children of men according to the kind of spirit which they possess.

"From the God of Knowledge comes all that is and shall be. Before ever they existed He established their whole design, and when, as ordained for them, they come into being, it is in accord with His glorious design that they accomplish their task without change. The laws of all things are in His hand and He provides them with all their needs.

"He has created man to govern the world, and has appointed for him two spirits in which to walk until the time of His visitation: the spirits of truth and falsehood. Those born of truth spring from a fountain of light, but those born of falsehood spring from a source of darkness. All the children of righteousness are ruled by the Prince of Light and walk in the ways of light, but all the children of falsehood are ruled by the Angel of Darkness and walk in the ways of darkness.

"The Angel of Darkness leads all the children of righteousness astray, and until his end, all their sin, iniquities, wickedness, and all their unlawful deeds are caused by his dominion in accordance with the mysteries of God. Every one of their chastisements, and every one of the seasons of their distress, shall be brought about by the rule of his persecution; for all his allotted spirits seek the overthrow of the sons of light.

"But the God of Israel and His Angel of Truth will succour all the sons of light. For it is He who created the spirits of Light and Darkness and founded every action upon them and established every deed upon their ways. And He loves the one everlastingly and delights in its works forever; but the counsel of the other He loathes and forever hates its ways.

"The nature of all the children of men is ruled by these two spirits, and during their life all the hosts of men have a portion in their divisions and walk in both their ways. And the whole reward for their deeds shall be, for everlasting ages, according to whether each man's portion in their two divisions is great or small. For God has established the spirits in equal measure until the final age, and has set everlasting hatred between their divisions. Truth abhors the works of falsehood, and falsehood hates all the ways of truth. And their struggle is fierce in all their arguments for they do not walk together.

"But in the mysteries of His understanding, and in His glorious wisdom, God has ordained an end for falsehood, and at the time of the visitation He will destroy it forever. Then truth, which has wallowed in the ways of wickedness during the dominion of falsehood until the appointed time of judgment, shall arise in the world forever. God will then purify every deed of Man with his truth; He will refine for Himself the human frame by rooting out all spirit of falsehood from the bounds of his flesh. Like purifying waters He will shed upon him the spirit of truth to cleanse him of all abomination and falsehood. And he shall be plunged into the spirit of purification that he may instruct the upright in the knowledge of the Most High and teach the wisdom of the sons of heaven to the perfect way. For God has chosen them for an everlasting Covenant and all the glory of Adam shall be theirs. There shall be no more lies and all the works of falsehood shall be put to shame."

D. Community Rule

This section contains the Community Rules of Conduct. The members are to be exclusive and avoid contact with the froward. The priests are to be the sons of Zadok, the only legitimate priests. They shall settle all matters of controversy. The members took an oath when they were initiated. Other than this, their attitude toward oaths was the same as that expressed by Jesus in his Sermon on the Mount.[6] They also held the view that the mere fact of washing cannot bring purification from sin unless there is repentance.

"And this is the Rule for the men of the Community who have freely pledged themselves to be converted from all evil and to cling to all His commandments according to His will.

"They shall separate from the congregation of the men of falsehood and shall unite, with respect to the Law and possessions, under the authority of the sons of Zadok, the Priests who keep the Covenant, and of the multitude of the men of the Community who hold fast to the Covenant. Every decision concerning doctrine, property, and justice shall be determined by them.

"They shall practice truth and humility in common, and justice and uprightness and charity and modesty in all their ways. No man shall walk in the stubbornness of his heart so that he strays after his heart and eyes and evil inclination, but he shall circumcise in the Community the foreskin of evil inclination and of stiffness of neck that they may lay a foundation of truth for Israel, for the Community of the everlasting Covenant.

"On joining the Community, this shall be their code of behavior with respect to all these precepts.

"Whoever approaches the Council of the Community shall enter the Covenant of God in the presence of all who have freely pledged themselves. He shall undertake by a binding oath to return with all his heart and soul to every commandment of the Law of Moses in accordance with all that has been revealed of it to the sons of Zadok, the Keepers of the Covenant and Seekers of His will.

"They shall not enter the water to partake of the pure Meal of the saints, for they shall not be cleansed unless they turn from their wickedness: for all who transgress His word are unclean. Likewise, no man shall consort with him with regard to his work or property lest he be burdened with the guilt of his sin. He shall indeed keep away from him in all things; as it is written, 'Keep away from all that is false'."

E. Assembly Rule

"Let not the sun go down on your wrath," is wise advice about not nursing a grudge. These words resemble those of both Jesus and of St. Paul. When 10 or more are present in a group, they must be led by a trained initiate. The insistence on rank and acknowledgement of each individual's position carry through all the rigid rules at Qumran. The hand of the priest will first invoke his blessing on the wine and bread of the Communion. The Communion dinner is preceded by washing and required a presence of a priest and a quorum of ten men which was the minimum number for a service.

"They shall rebuke one another in truth, humility, and charity. Let no man address his companion with anger, or ill-temper, or obduracy, or with envy prompted by the spirit of wickedness. Let him not hate him because of his uncircumcised heart, but let him rebuke him on the very same day lest he incur guilt because of him. And furthermore, let no man accuse his companion before the congregation without having first admonished him in the presence of witnesses.

"These are the ways in which all of them shall walk, each man with his companion, wherever they dwell.

"The man of lesser rank shall obey the greater in matters of work and money.

"They shall eat in common and pray in common and deliberate in common.

"Wherever there are ten men of the Council of the Community there shall not lack a Priest among them. And they shall all sit before him according to their rank and shall be asked their counsel in all things in that order. And when the table has been prepared for eating, and the new wine for drinking, the Priest shall be the first to stretch out his hand to bless the first-fruits of the bread and wine.

"And where the ten are, there shall never lack a man among them who shall study the Law continually, day and night, concerning the right conduct of a man with his companion.

"This is the Rule for an Assembly of the Congregation. Each man shall sit in his place: the Priests shall sit first, and the elders second, and all the rest of the people according to their rank, each man bringing his knowledge to the Council of the Community.

"No man shall interrupt a companion before his speech has ended, nor speak before a man of higher rank, each man shall speak in his turn."

F. Initiation of Full Members

The rules for entering the Community require the initiate to go through two years of training during which time his property will be put away and neither will he enjoy the Community's property. He is then examined and if it is deemed that he enter the Community, he takes his place among his brethren according to his rank.[7]

"Every man, born of Israel, who freely pledges himself to join the Council of the Community,[8] shall be examined by the Guardian of the head of the Congregation concerning his understanding and his deeds. If he is fitted to the discipline, he shall admit him into the Convenant that he may be converted to the truth and depart from all falsehood; and he shall instruct him in all the rules of the Community. And later, when he comes to stand before the Congregation, they shall all deliberate his case, and according to the decision of the Council of the Congregation he shall either enter or depart. After he has entered the Council of the Community he shall not touch the pure Meal of the Congregation until one full year is completed, and until he has been examined concerning his spirit and deeds; nor shall he have any share of the property of the Congregation. Then when he has completed one year with the Community, the Congregation shall deliberate his case with regard to his understanding and observance of the Law. And if it be his destiny, according to the judgment of the Priests and the multitude of the men of their Covenant, to enter the company of the Community, his property and earnings shall be handed over to the Bursar of the Congregation who shall register it to his account and shall not spend it for the Congregation. He shall not touch the Drink of the Congregation until he has completed a second year among the men of the Community. But when the second year has passed, he shall be examined, and if it be his destiny, according to the judgment of the Congregation, to enter the Community, then he shall be inscribed among his brethren in the order of his rank for the Law, and for justice, and for the pure Meal; his property shall be merged and he shall offer his counsel and judgment to the Community."

G. Rules of Conduct

These are the Rules in which the Community will judge an individual at a court of inquiry. The rules are severe and meticulous.

"These are the Rules by which they shall judge at a Community Court of Inquiry according to the cases. If one of them has lied deliberately in matters of property, he shall be excluded from the pure Meal of the Congregation for one year and shall do penance with respect to one quarter of his food.

"Whoever has answered his companion with obstinacy, or has addressed him impatiently, going so far as to take no account of the dignity of his fellow by disobeying the order of a brother inscribed before him, he has taken the law into his own hand; therefore he shall do penance for one year and shall be excluded.

"If any man has uttered the Most Venerable Name even though frivolously, or as a result of shock or for any other reason whatever, while reading the Book or praying, he shall be dismissed and shall return to the Council of the Community no more.

"If he has spoken in anger against one of the Priests inscribed in the Book, he shall do penance for one year and shall be excluded for his soul's sake from the pure Meal of the Congregation. But if he has spoken unwittingly, he shall do penance for six months.

"Whoever has spoken foolishly: three months.

"Whoever has interrupted his companion whilst speaking: ten days.

"Whoever has lain down to sleep during an Assembly of

the Congregation: thirty days. And likewise, whoever has left, without reason, an Assembly of the Congregation as many as three times during one Assembly, shall do penance for ten days. But if he has departed whilst they were standing he shall do penance for thirty days.

"Whoever has gone naked before his companion, without having been obliged to do so, he shall do penance for six months.

"Whoever has spat in an Assembly of the Congregation shall do penance for thirty days.

"Whoever has been so poorly dressed that when drawing his hand from beneath his garment his nakedness has been seen, he shall do penance for thirty days.

"Whoever has guffawed foolishly shall do penance for thirty days.

"Whoever has drawn out his left hand to gesticulate with it shall do penance for ten days.

"Whoever has gone about slandering his companion shall be excluded from the pure Meal of the Congregation for one year and shall do penance. But whoever has slandered the Congregation shall be expelled from amongst them and shall return no more.

"Whoever has murmured against the authority of the Community shall be expelled and shall not return."

H. Priestly Duties and the Coming of the Prophet

The priests of Qumran used 12 laymen for probably the same reason the early church had 12 apostles — both represented the 12 tribes of Israel. The Covenant also used three priests — this was later adopted by the church as their three "Pillars."

The "coming of the Prophet" is a direct reference to Deuteronomy 18:17-18: "And the Lord said unto me...I will raise them up a Prophet from among their brethren, like unto thee, and will put words in his mouth."

In the New Age, the Messiah of Aaron who will act as high priest and the Messiah of Israel who will be anointed as king will gather the triumphant forces after the defeat of Belial. The Prophet or Forerunner was most often associated with Elijah.

"In the Council of the Community there shall be twelve men and three Priests, perfectly versed in all that is revealed of the Law, whose works shall be truth, righteousness, justice, loving kindness, and humility.

"Every man who enters the Council of Holiness, the Council of those who walk in the way of perfection as commanded by God, and who deliberately or through negligence transgresses one word of the Law of Moses, or any point whatever, shall be expelled from the Council of the Community and shall return no more. But if he has acted inadvertently, he shall be excluded from the pure Meal and the Council.

"The sons of Aaron alone shall command in matters of justice and property, and every rule concerning the men of the Community shall be determined according to their word.

"As for the property of the men of holiness who walk in perfection, it shall not be merged. As for the property of the men of holiness with that of the men of falsehood who have not purified their life by separating themselves from iniquity and walking in the way of perfection. They shall depart from none of the counsels of the Law to walk in the stubbornness of their hearts, but shall be ruled by the primitive precepts in which the men of the Community were first instructed until there shall come the Prophet and the Messiahs of Aaron and Israel."

THE DAMASCUS DOCUMENT

When scholars read the Manual of Discipline, they discovered a strong similarity to a manuscript known as the Damascus Document that had been found in 1896 in a geniza of an old synagogue in Cairo. Two documents, one dating from the tenth century A.D. and one from the twelfth century A.D. are copies of an earlier Damascus Document that came from the Caves at Qumran. The title "Damascus Document" is derived

60

from the exhortation to enter a "New Covenant" in "the Land of Damascus" when the faithful Israelites left the Temple of Jerusalem and fled into the desert.

The Damascus Document, translated by G. Vermes, is divided into the Exhortation, in which the Guardian of the Community tries to encourage his followers to remain faithful, and a list of statutes. It contains a collection of laws that relate to vows, oaths, tribunals, purification, the Sabbath, and the distinction between purity and impurity for those who live in cities and camps.

The guardian is probably the Teacher of Righteousness who came into the Community and gave it a sense of direction. Most scholars subscribe to the fact that it was written by the Teacher, although no direct mention is made of himself or his name.

A. The Survival of the Remnant

God did not deliver Israel to be destroyed, but delivered the faithful Remnant into the desert some 390 years after He had delivered them into the hands of Nebuchadnezzar. They groped their way for the first 20 years until the Teacher of Righteousness appeared to lead them in the way of God's heart.

"Hear now, all you who enter the Covenant, and I will unstop your ears concerning the ways of the wicked. Destruction towards those who depart from the way and abhor the Precept. They shall have no remnant or survivor. For from the beginning God chose them not; He knew their deeds before ever they were created and He hated their generations, and He hid his face from the Land until they were consumed. For He knew the years of their coming and the length and exact duration of their times for all ages to come and throughout eternity.

"Those who hold fast to it are destined to live forever and all the glory of Adam shall be theirs. As God ordained for them by the hand of the Prophet Ezekiel, saying, The Priests, the Levites, and the sons of Zadok who kept the charge of my sanctuary when the children of Israel strayed from me, they shall offer me fat and blood.

"The sons of Zadok are the elect of Israel, the men called by name who shall stand at the end of days."

B. The Duties of the Essenes

These instructions were for those who lived in the small communities and in camps. They are admonished to keep away from the unclean. Unlike the monks at Qumran, they came in contact with the world. Some discouraged marriage, some did not. Note that the followers are instructed to keep the Sabbath according to its exact interpretation. Each man shall love his brother as himself. He may marry and live according to the Law.

"None of those brought into the Covenant shall enter the Temple to light His altar in vain. They shall bar the door, forasmuch as God said, 'Who among you will bar its door?' And, 'You shall not light my altar in vain.' They shall take care to act according to the exact interpretation of the Law during the age of wickedness. They shall separate from the sons of the Pit, and shall keep away from the unclean riches of wickedness acquired by vow or anathema or from the Temple treasure; they shall not rob the poor of His people, to make of widows their prey and of the fatherless their victim. They shall distinguish between clean and unclean, and shall proclaim the difference between holy and profane. They shall keep the Sabbath day according to its exact interpretation, and the feasts and the Day of Fasting according to the finding of the members of the New Covenant in the Land of Damascus. They shall set aside the holy things according to the exact teaching concerning them. They shall love each man his brother as himself.

"And if they live in camps according to the rule of the Land as it was from ancient times, marrying according to the custom of the Law and begetting children, they shall walk according to the Law."

62

C. The New Covenant in Damascus

The Community went into exile and was led by their Teacher of Righteousness. Between the times of the "gathering in" of the Teacher, which suggests a natural death, and the time of the Messiahs of Aaron and Israel, those who abandoned the Covenant were repudiated by the Community. The Man of Falsehood is the Wicked Priest. The time "forty years" after the Teacher's death signifies a holy number as a sign from God.

"None of the men who enter the New Covenant in the Land of Damascus, and who again betray it and depart from the fountain of living waters, shall be reckoned with the Council of the people or inscribed in its Book from the day of gathering in of the Teacher of the Community until the coming of the Messiah out of Aaron and Israel.

"And thus shall it be for every man who enters the congregation of men of perfect holiness but faints in performing the duties of the upright.

"They shall be judged in the same manner as their companions were judged who deserted to the Scoffers. For they have spoken wrongly against the precepts of righteousness, and have despised the Covenant and the Pact – The New Covenant – which they made in the Land of Damascus. Neither they nor their kin shall have any part in the house of the Law.

"From the day of the gathering in of the Unique Teacher of the Community until the consuming of all men of war who deserted to the Man of Falsehood there shall pass about forty years. And during that age the wrath of God shall be kindled against Israel; as He said, 'There shall be no king, no prince, no judge, no man to rebuke with justice.'

"But all those who hold fast to these precepts, going and coming in accordance with the Law, who heed the voice of the Teacher, they shall rejoice and their hearts shall be strong, and they shall prevail over all the sons of the earth. God will forgive them and they shall see His salvation because they took refuge in His holy Name."

D. Codes for Urban Communities

These codes are the strict regulations for the Covenanters who lived in contact with the Gentiles. The restrictions put on the celebration of the Sabbath are as strict as any of those practiced by the priests at Qumran. Man must remain idle on the Sabbath. Only in case of a life threatening situation can one be permitted to perform any act to assist the threatened.

"And this is the Rule for the Judges of the Congregation. Ten shall be elected from the congregation for a definite time, four from the tribe of Levi and Aaron, and six from Israel. They shall be learned in the Book of Meditation and in the constitutions of the Covenant, and aged between twenty-five and sixty years. No man over the age of sixty shall hold office as a Judge of the Congregation, for because man sinned his days have been shortened, and in the heat of His anger against the inhabitants of the earth God ordained that their understanding should depart even before their days are completed.

"Concerning the Sabbath to observe it according to its law. No man shall work on the sixth day from the moment when the sun's orb is distant by its own fullness from the gate wherein it sinks;[9] for this is what He said, 'Observe the Sabbath day to keep it holy.' No man shall speak any vain or idle word on the Sabbath day. He shall make no loan to his companion. He shall make no decision in matters of money and gain. He shall say nothing about work or labor to be done on the morrow.

"No man shall walk abroad to do business on the Sabbath. He shall not walk more than one thousand cubits beyond his town.

"No man shall eat on the Sabbath day except that which is already prepared. He shall eat nothing lying in the fields. He shall not drink except in the camp. If he is on a journey and goes down to bathe, he shall drink where he stands, but he shall not draw water into a vessel.

"No man shall walk more than two thousand cubits after a beast to pasture it outside his town. He shall not raise his hand to strike it with his fist.

"No man shall take anything out of the house or bring anything in. He shall lift neither sand nor dust in his dwelling. No foster-father shall carry a child whilst going and coming on the Sabbath.

"No man shall assist a beast to give birth on the Sabbath day. And if it should fall into a cistern or pit, he shall not lift it out on the Sabbath. But should any man fall into water or fire, let him be pulled out with the aid of a ladder or rope or some such tool.

"No man entering the house of worship shall come unclean and in need of washing. And at the sounding of the trumpets for assembly, he shall go there before or after the meeting, and shall not cause the whole service to stop, for it is a holy service.

"They shall eat no fish unless split alive and their blood poured out. And as for locusts, according to their various kinds they shall plunge them alive into water, for this is what their nature requires.

"All wood and stones and dust defiled by the impurity of a man shall be reckoned like men with regard to conveying defilement; whoever touches them shall be defiled by their defilement. And every nail or peg in the wall of a house in which a dead man lies shall become unclean as any working tool becomes unclean.

"The Rule for the assembly of the towns shall be according to these precepts that they may distinguish between unclean and clean, and discriminate between the holy and the profane.

"And these are the precepts in which the Master shall walk in his commerce with all the living in accordance with the statute proper to every age. And in accordance with this statute shall the seed of Israel walk and they shall not be cursed."

E. Rules for the Assembly and Guardian of the Camp
"And where the ten are, there shall never be lacking a Priest learned in the Book of Meditation; they shall all be ruled by him.

"But should he not be experienced in these matters, where as one of the Levites is experienced in them, then it shall be determined that all the members of the camp shall go and come according to the latter's word.

"But should there be a case of applying the law of leprosy to a man, then the Priest shall come and shall stand in the camp and the Guardian shall instruct him in the exact interpretation of the Law.

"Even if the Priest is a simpleton, it is he who shall lock up the leper; for theirs is the judgment.

"This is the Rule for the Guardian of the Camp. He shall instruct the Congregation in the works of God. He shall cause them to consider His mighty deeds and shall recount them as a father loves his children, and shall carry them in all their distress like a shepherd his sheep.

"He shall examine every man entering his Congregation with regard to his deeds, understanding, strength, ability, and possessions, and shall inscribe him in his place according to his rank in the lot of Light.

"No member of the camp shall have authority to admit a man to the Congregation against the decision of the Guardian of the Camp.

"The Rule for the assembly of all the camps. They shall all be enrolled by name: first the Priests, second the Levites, third the Israelites, and fourth the proselytes. And thus shall they sit and thus be questioned on all matters. And the Priest who enrolls the Congregation shall be from thirty to sixty years old, learned in the Book of Meditation and in all the judgment of the Law so as to pronounce them correctly.

"The Guardian of all the camps shall be from thirty to fifty years old, one who has mastered all the secrets of men and the languages of all their clans. Whoever enters the Congregation shall do so according to his word, each in his rank, and whoever has anything to say with regard to any suit or judgment, let him say it to the Guardian."

THE WAR BETWEEN THE SONS OF LIGHT AND THE SONS OF DARKNESS

This is the manual that describes the final war between the Essenes and the "Kittim," or the Romans. The war is to last a total of 40 years and be waged against the whole Gentile world. It contains a long list of rules for the military and religious preparation and the conduct of the fighting. The War Scroll, which is translated by G. Vermes, corresponds to the art of war that was practiced by the Roman Legion. Perhaps the priests of Qumran used a Roman military manual as a pattern for their own rules and strategy. The square shields, the foot soldier, the buckler of the horseman and the battle array of three lines are all characteristically Roman. This, as well as the general representation that the Kittim were masters of the world, placed the date of this composition as somewhere in the last decades of the first century B.C. or at the beginning of the first century A.D.

The manual is more than a set of rules for military warfare. It is a theological struggle between the forces of Light and Darkness. The duration of the battle is predetermined as are its phases and outcome. The two opposing forces are evenly matched and only the hand of God can put the victory on the side of the Sons of Light when he deals His final blow to Satan and his kingdom.

A. The First Engagement

The first battle between the Sons of Light and the Sons of Darkness shall attack Edom, Moab, the Ammonites and the Philistine area, the Kittim of Assyria, and all the violators of the Covenant who give them aid. The Sons of Light will return from the desert to Jerusalem and the children of Levi, Judah, and Benjamin who are among those exiles shall wage war against these peoples.

B. The Mobilization

Preparation for the final battle was to begin seven years

prior to the beginning of the war. Hopefully, Belial would not use his knowledge or intelligence to strike before his opponents had finished their lengthy preparations. They were preparing for a long war and they needed time to ready themselves. All their trumpets had their slogans upon them. "The Enlisted of God" was to be inscribed on the trumpets of assembly. The trumpets of ambush would be given the inscription: "The hidden powers of God are able to destroy wickedness." "God has smitten all the children of Darkness, He will not turn back His anger until He has consumed them," was the inscription for the trumpets of pursuit.

Each section in the attack would have an inscription on its standards. Platoons would have: "Finished is the stand of the froward through the mighty acts of God," on their standards. Battalion commanders used: "God's anger is vented in fury against Belial and against all that cast their lot with him, that they have no remnant." The standard of the general would be inscribed: "They are to write his name and the names of Israel and Levi and Aaron, and the name of the twelve tribes of Israel" along with the names of the commanding officers of each tribe.

C. Weapons and Battle Formations

Shields would measure 2 1/2 cubits long by 2 1/2 cubits wide. They would be highly polished bronze to shine like a mirror. The spears would be 7 cubits long, "with the blade and point 1/14 of the whole."

The main formations would be:

1. A straight line flanked by towers.
2. A concave line flanked by towers.
3. A convex line flanked by towers.
4. A slightly convex curve, with spearhead columns in advance on the flanks.
5. A slightly concave curve, with wings of cavalry in advance on both flanks. No mention is made as to how the towers are to be deployed.

D. The Combatants

Combatants are described in this strange war and are somewhat unexpected.

"The horses advancing into battle with the foot-soldiers shall be stallions; they shall be swift, sensitive of mouth, and sound of wind, and of the required age, trained for war, and accustomed to noise and to every kind of sight. Their riders shall be gallant fighting men and skilled horsemen, and their age shall be from thirty to forty-five years.

"The men of the army shall be from forty to fifty years old.

"The inspectors of the camps shall be from fifty to sixty years old.

"The officers shall be from forty to fifty years old.

"The despoilers of the slain, the plunderers of booty, the cleansers of the land, the keepers of the baggage, and those who furnish the provisions shall be from twenty-five to thirty years old. No boy or woman shall enter their camp from the time they leave Jerusalem and march out to war until they return. No man who is lame, or blind, or crippled, or afflicted with a lasting bodily blemish, or smitten with a bodily impurity, none of these shall march out to war with them. They shall all be freely enlisted for war, perfect in spirit and body and prepared for the Day of Vengeance."

E. The Battle Begins

"When the battle formations are marshalled facing the enemy, formation facing formation, seven Priests of the sons of Aaron shall advance from the middle gates to the place between formations. They shall be clothed in vestments of white cloth of flax, in a fine linen tunic and fine linen breeches; and they shall be girdled with fine cloth of flax embroidered with blue, purple, and scarlet thread, a many-colored design worked by a craftsman. And on their heads they shall wear mitred turbans.

"The trumpets shall sound to direct the slingers until they

have cast seven times. Afterwards, the Priests shall sound for them the trumpets of withdrawal and they shall return to the flank of the first formation to take up their position.

"Then the Priests shall sound the trumpets of Summons and three divisions of foot-soldiers shall advance from the gates and shall station themselves between the formations; the horsemen shall be on their flanks, to the right and to the left. The Priest shall sound a sustained blast on the trumpets for battle array. And the Priests shall then blow a shrill staccato blast on the six trumpets of Massacre to direct the battle, and the Levites and all the blowers of ram's horns shall sound a mighty alarm to terrify the heart of the enemy, and therewith the javelins shall fly out to bring down the slain. Then the sound of the horns shall cease, but the Priests shall continue to blow a shrill staccato blast on the trumpets to direct the battle until they have thrown seven times against the enemy formation.

"And the Levites and all the blowers of rams' horns shall sound an alarm, a mighty blast, and therewith they shall set about to bring down the slain with their hands. All the people shall cease their clamor but the Priests shall continue to blow the trumpets of Massacre to direct the battle until the enemy is smitten and put to flight; and the Priests shall blow to direct the battle.

"And when they are smitten before them, the Priests shall sound the trumpets of Summons and all the foot soldiers shall rally to them from the midst of the front formations, and the six divisions, together with the fighting division, shall take up their stations.

"All these shall pursue the enemy to destroy him in an everlasting destruction in the battle of God. The Priests shall sound for them the trumpets of Pursuit, and they shall deploy against all the enemy in a pursuit to destruction; and the horsemen shall thrust them back on the flanks of the battle until they are utterly destroyed.

"And as the slain men fall, the Priests shall trumpet from afar; they shall not approach the slain lest they be defiled with unclean blood. For they are holy, and they shall not profane

70

the anointing of their priesthood with the blood of nations of vanity."

F. The Final Triumph

After the final battle, the enemy lays slain before the triumphant Covenanters and God's peace reigns on the battlefield.

"And when they have risen from the slain to return to the camp, they shall sing the Psalm of Return. And in the morning, they shall wash their garments, and shall cleanse themselves of the blood of the bodies of the ungodly. And they shall return to the positions in which they stood in battle formation before the fall of the enemy slain, and these they shall all bless the God of Israel. Rejoicing together, they shall praise His Name, and speaking they shall say:

'Blessed be the God of Israel
   Who keeps mercy towards His Covenant,
And the appointed times of salvation
   with the people He has delivered!' "

For the Covenanters, the God of Israel, Who created the Universe and all that it encompasses, was their own personal God. He had the power to overcome all gods of all other nations and to conquer their governments as well. It may be difficult to understand how they could be serious about such a plan, but the tribes of Israel had defeated great numbers of enemies before with the help of God. They had won against overwhelming odds, as David did against Goliath of Gath. Surely they believed that their lives were the work of God; that they were performing His will. They were counting on His intervention. With the hand of God, and if they carried out exactly what they believed to be His plan, what may seem as dreamlike optimism would be brought to pass. It would take such a miraculous act to bring about the End of Days and establish a new order in the kingdom.

THE THANKSGIVING HYMNS

The Hymns Scroll came out of Cave I where it suffered much deterioration. The first translation was published by E. L. Sukenik. He reported difficulty not only in understanding the sense of the poems, but also where one poem ends and the next begins. A translation by G. Vermes contains 25 compositions similar to the biblical Psalms. It contains prayers, Hymns of Thanksgiving, and a variety of spiritual and doctrinal material. The author is thankful to God for having been saved from the lot of the wicked. He believes that he is God's choice and has been singled out by his Maker and given divine knowledge of which he is unworthy.

Some of the hymns raise sentiments and thoughts that are common to the Community, while others refer to a teacher who appeared to lead and was abandoned by his friends and persecuted by his enemies. Several scholars tend to attribute the Hymns Scroll as the work of one man, the Teacher of Righteousness, although he is never acknowledged nor is even a reference made to his name in the writing.

A. The Hymn for Initiation

In the wisdom of Thy knowledge Thou didst
    establish their destiny before even they were.
All things exist according to Thy will
    and without Thee nothing is done.

These things I know
    by the wisdom which comes from Thee,
for Thou hast unstopped my ears
    to marvelous mysteries.

And yet I, shape of clay
    kneaded in water,
a ground of shame
    and a source of pollution,

a melting-pot of wickedness
  and an edifice of sin,
a straying and perverted spirit
  of no understanding,
  fearful of righteous judgments,
what can I say that is not foreknown,
  and what can I utter that is not foretold?
All things are graven before Thee
  on a written Reminder
  for everlasting ages,
and for the numbered cycles
  of the eternal years
  in all their seasons;
they are not hidden or absent from Thee.

What shall a man say
  concerning his sin?
and how shall he plead
  concerning his iniquities?
And how shall he reply
  to righteous judgment?
For thine, O God of knowledge,
  are all righteous deeds
  and the Counsel of truth.

B. Delivered from the Throes of Death

For the children have come to the throes of Death
  and she labors in her pains who bears the Man.
For amid the throes of Death
  she shall bring forth a man-child,
and amid the pains of Hell
  there shall spring from her child-bearing crucible
  a Marvelous Mighty Counsellor;
and the Man shall be delivered
  from out of the throes.

When he is conceived
    all wombs shall quicken,
and the time of their delivery
    shall be in grievous pains;
they shall be appalled who are with child.
And when he is brought forth
    every pang shall come upon
    the child-bearing crucible.

C) Raised to Everlasting Height

I thank Thee, O Lord,
    for Thou hast redeemed my soul from the Pit,
and from the Hell of Abaddon
    Thou hast raised me up to everlasting height.

I walk on limitless level ground,
and I know there is hope for him
    whom Thou hast shaped from dust
    for the everlasting Council.
Thou hast cleansed a perverse spirit of great sin
    that it may stand with the host of the Holy Ones,
and that it may enter into community
    with the congregation of the Sons of Heaven.
Thou hast allotted to man an everlasting destiny
    amidst the spirits of knowledge,
that he may praise Thy Name in a common rejoicing
    and recount Thy marvels before all Thy works.

D. Thou Manifest Thyself Through Me

Clinging to Thee, I will stand.
I will rise against those who despise me
    and my hand shall be turned
    against those who deride me;
for they have no esteem for me
    that Thou mayest manifest Thy might through me.

Thou hast revealed Thyself to me in Thy power
    as perfect Light,
    and Thou hast not covered my face with shame.
All those who are gathered
    in Thy Covenant
    inquire of me,
and they hearken to me who walk
    in the way of Thy heart,
    who array themselves for Thee
    in the Council of the holy.

Through me Thou hast illumined
    the face of the Congregation
    and hast shown thine infinite power.
For Thou hast given me knowledge
    through Thy marvellous mysteries,
and hast shown Thyself mighty within me
    in the midst of Thy marvellous Council.
Thou hast done wonders before the Congregation
    for the sake of Thy glory,
that they may make known Thy mighty deeds
    to all the living.

E. Thou Hast not Abandoned Me

I thank Thee O Lord,
    for Thou hast not abandoned me
    whilst I sojourned among a people burdened within.

Thou hast not judged me
    according to my guilt,
    nor hast Thou abandoned me
    because of the designs of my inclination;
but Thou hast saved my life from the Pit.

Thou hast confirmed the counsel of truth in my heart
    and the waters of the Covenant for those who seek it.

Thou hast closed up the mouth of the young lions
　　whose teeth are like a sword,
　　and whose great teeth are like a pointed spear,
　　like the venom of dragons.
All their design is for robbery
　　and they have lain in wait;
but they have not opened their mouth against me.

Thou hast dealt wondrously with the poor one
　　to manifest Thy might within me
　　in the presence of the sons of men.
Thou hast placed him in the melting-pot,
　　like gold in the fire,
and like silver refined
　　in the melting-pot of the smelters,
　　to be purified seven times.
The wicked and fierce have stormed against me
　　with their afflictions;
　　they have pounded my soul all day.
But Thou, O my God,
hast changed the tempest to a breeze.

F. Beside a Watered Garden in a Wilderness

I thank Thee, O Lord,
　　for Thou hast placed me beside a fountain of streams
　　in an arid land,
and close to a spring of waters
　　in a dry land,
and beside a watered garden
　　in a wilderness.

For Thou didst set a plantation
　　of cypress, pine, and cedar for Thy glory,
trees of life beside a mysterious fountain
　　hidden among the trees by the water,
and they put out a shoot of the everlasting Plant.

But before they did so, they took root
and sent out their roots to the watercourse
that its stem might be open to the living waters
and be one with the everlasting spring.

Thou didst hedge in its fruit, God,
with the mystery of mighty Heroes
and of spirits of holiness
and of the whirling flame of fire.
No man shall approach the well-spring of life
or drink the waters of holiness
with the everlasting trees,
or bear fruit with the Plant of heaven,
who seeing hast not discerned,
and considering hast not believed
in the fountain of life,
who hast turned his hand against the everlasting bud.

G. Thou Has Delighted Me with thy Holy Spirit

For Thou hast known me
from the time of my father,
and hast chosen me from the womb.
From the belly of my mother
Thou hast dealt kindly with me,
and from the breast of her who conceived me
have Thy mercies been with me.
Thy grace was with me in the lap of her who reared me,
and from my youth
Thou hast illumined me
with the wisdom of Thy judgment.

Thou hast upheld me with certain truth;
Thou hast delighted me with Thy Holy Spirit
and hast opened my heart till this day.
For my father knew me not
and my mother abandoned me to Thee.

For Thou art a father to all the sons of Thy truth,
    so dost Thou rejoice in them;
and as a foster-father bearing a child in his lap,
    so carest Thou for all Thy creatures.

What then is man that is earth,
    that is shaped from clay and returns to the dust,
that Thou shouldst give him to understand such marvels
    and make known to him the counsel of Thy truth?

Clay and dust that I am,
    what can I devise unless Thou wish it,
    and what contrive unless Thou desire it?
What strength shall I have
    unless Thou keep me upright,
and how shall I understand
    unless by the spirit which Thou hast shaped for me?
What can I say unless Thou open my mouth
    and how can I answer unless Thou enlighten me?

Behold, Thou are Prince of gods
    and King of majesties,
Lord of all spirits,
    and Ruler of all creatures;
nothing is done without Thee,
    and nothing is known without Thy will.
Beside Thee there is nothing,
    and nothing can compare with Thee in strength;
in the presence of Thy glory there is nothing,
    and Thy might is without price.

H. Enter Into a Covenant With Thee

Blessed art Thou, O Lord,
    who hast given understanding
How shall I look, unless Thou open my eyes?
    Or hear, unless Thou unstop my ears?

I know it is for Thyself
   that Thou hast done these things, O God;
It is Thy purpose to do mightily
   and to establish all things
   for Thy glory.
For what am I reckoned to be worthy of this?
For into an ear of dust
   Thou hast put a new word
   and hast engraved on a heart of stone
   things everlasting.
Thou hast caused the straying spirit to return
   that it may enter into a Covenant with Thee,
and stand before Thee forever
   in the everlasting abode,
illumined with perfect Light forever,
   with no more darkness,
for unending seasons of joy
and unnumbered ages of peace.

THE MESSIANIC RULE

This scroll is a vivid portrait of the Messianic Banquet that is to take place at the End of Days. The full assembly takes place when God brings the Messiah with them. Messiah literally means "the Anointed One." The Brotherhood expected two messiahs — one priestly and one princely. The priestly messiah held precedence over the princely messiah. This division of high priest and king runs throughout Jewish tradition. The translation of the scroll is by G. Vermes.

The Congregation fully expected that the Messiah of Israel would be sent by God. The Congregation would gather for their triumphant meal with the high priest, the Messiah of Aaron, seated at the head of the Banquet. Each person would be seated before him in accordance with his rank. Note that the Messiah of Israel is not the head of the Banquet, but must bow down to the high priest, the Messiah of Aaron. The high priest is still superior to the anointed king.

79

"This is the Rule for all the Congregation of Israel in the last days, when they shall join the Community to walk according to the law of the sons of Zadok, the Priests, and of the men of their Covenant, who have turned aside from the way of the people, the men of His Council who keep His Covenant in the midst of iniquity, offering expiation for the Land. When they come, they shall summon them all, the little children and the women also, and they shall read into their ears the precepts of the Covenant and shall expound to them all their statutes that they may no longer stray in their errors.

"And no man smitten with any human uncleanliess shall enter the assembly of God; no man smitten with any of them shall be confirmed in his office in the congregation. No man smitten in his flesh, or paralyzed in his feet or hands, or lame, or blind, or deaf, or dumb, or smitten in his flesh with a visible blemish; no old and tottery man unable to stay still in the midst of the Congregation; none of these shall come to hold office among the Congregation of the men of renown, for the Angels of Holiness are with their congregation. Should one of them have something to say to the Council of Holiness, let him be questioned privately; but let him not enter among the Congregation for he is smitten.

"This shall be the assembly of the men of renown called to the meeting of the Council of the Community when Priest Messiah shall summon them. He shall come at the head of the whole congregation of Israel with all his brethren, the sons of Aaron, the Priests, those called to the assembly, the men of renown; and they shall sit before him, each man in the order of his dignity. And then the Messiah of Israel shall come, and the chiefs of the clans of Israel shall sit before him, each in the order of his dignity, according to his place in their camps and marches. And before them shall sit all the heads of family of the congregation, and the wise men of the holy congregation, each in the order of his dignity. And when they shall gather for the common table to eat and drink new wine, when the common table shall be set for eating and the new wine poured for drinking, let no men extend his hand over the first-fruits of bread and wine before the Priest; for it is he who shall bless the first-fruits of bread and wine, and shall be the first to extend his hand over the bread. Thereafter, the Messiah of Israel shall extend his hand over the bread, and all the congregation of the Community shall utter a blessing, each man in the order of his dignity.

"It is according to this statute that they shall proceed at every meal at which at least ten men are gathered together."

10

The Second Battle of the Scrolls

The first Battle of the Scrolls is over. The scrolls are accepted as authentic writings dating well before any other biblical manuscripts that exist today. There is complete evidence for dating these manuscripts between 150 B.C. and A.D. 70 and for their source being the Essene Monastery of Qumran. A second battle over the scrolls took place in the mid-1950s. Due to some hypothesizing by different scholars and writers, the first attempt was made to Christianize the scrolls and to "Essenize" Christianity. This then resulted in a tremendous backlash by organized religion and, even as of this writing, the pendulum has not begun to swing back toward a neutral position.

Although the scrolls were discovered next to the Dead Sea in 1947, it wasn't until 1955 that they were discovered in America. In May of that year, the *New Yorker magazine* dedicated its whole issue to an article about the Dead Sea Scrolls written by Edmund Wilson. The issue was a total sell out. He expanded his work into a book that became a best seller.

This hunger for information on the Dead Sea Scrolls was probably religious in origin. Many hoped the new discoveries would shed new light on the life of the noblest, most attractive hero in history. There was also a fascination generated from the romance of buried treasure and archaeological novelty. But the deeper interest in the scrolls among Christians probably resulted from a fear that their basic beliefs were being threatened, while some hostile agnostics hoped that finally Christianity might be proved wrong. Would the scrolls undermine the Gospels of Jesus or the interpretation of his story in the Christian Creeds?

The first doubts were raised by Dupont-Sommer in 1950. In his paper to the French Academy of Inscriptions which he later expanded into a book, he described Jesus as the "Teacher of Righteousness"[1] and he implied that Qumran was the cradle of Christianity. Dupont-Sommer describes the Teacher of Righteousness as Jesus in preaching penitence, poverty, humility, love of one's neighbor and chastity.

The Teacher and Jesus each prescribed the Law of Moses finished and perfected by their own revelations. And, as Jesus, the Teacher of Righteousness was the Elect, the Messiah of God, the Redeemer of the world. The Teacher was subjected to hostility by priests and the Sadducees, condemned and put to death.[2] He pronounced judgment on Jerusalem, was destroyed by the Romans, and at the End of Times, will return to judge the world. He founded his church in which the central rite is the sacrificial meal ministered by the priests and his followers awaited for his glorious return.[3] The head of the church was an overseer or bishop and the ideals of the church were unity, communion in love – even to the point of sharing community property.

One thing that Dupont-Sommer did not do was dwell on the differences between the Teacher of Righteousness and Jesus, of which there were many. The fact that in his similarities he describes the Teacher of Righteousness as the Messiah and the Redeemer of the world who was condemned and put to death; and that he points out Jerusalem was destroyed by the Romans for putting him to death, and that the Messiah or this Teacher will return and will be judge over all, are neither substantiated by history nor by the scrolls. The scrolls show that the Teacher of Righteousness was believed to be neither the Messiah nor the Redeemer. Dupont-Sommer's translations tend to read into them the points that he is trying to make and do not correspond with translations by other scholars.

In a 1955 *New Yorker magazine* article, Edmund Wilson detected a feeling of disturbance and even fear on the part of New Testament scholars. Wilson surmised that there was a suppressed implication on the part of scholars to take hold of the subject and place it in its historical perspective. He believed that there was an early attempt to date the scrolls very late to diminish their effect on Christianity. On this point, his concern for the integrity of the scholars was little more than ridiculous.

What Wilson did manage to do was to call attention to the scrolls in America and force the New Testament scholars working on the scrolls to come forth with more information and publications on their findings. There had not been much information coming forth prior to this from the scholars due to the great amount of effort and time it took to piece together huge puzzles and then to make interpretations on such a vast volume of documents. The disagreements between certain scholars in what they saw in the scrolls was viewed by Wilson as an attempt to suppress certain information that would damage the basic Christian doctrines. So the notion circulated that Christians were in confusion.

Wilson's article can be summed up with his suggestion that Christianity is simply an episode in human history, as opposed to the Church's view as it being a unique revelation of God's purpose. The Christian regards Christ's life on earth as taking place in a human episodical setting, about which he tries to learn as much as he possibly can. Nothing has emerged from the scrolls to change anything written in the Gospels about Christ's life on earth.

In 1956, John Allegro publicly discussed the Teacher of Righteousness. Allegro stated that the Teacher was handed over to the Wicked Priest, who he believed to be Alexander Jannaeus, and, "When his disciples took him down from the

85

cross, they reverently buried him and began to wait his return as the glorious Messiah." Allegro used the Commentary on Nahum as evidence of his belief. This scroll describes Alexander Jannaeus "hanging men on trees," a thing never done formerly in Israel. He interpreted this to mean that Jannaeus had crucified the Teacher of Righteousness.

The Commentary on Nahum refers to Alexander Jannaeus and his persecution of 800 Pharisees for their attempt to rebel against him and their aid to the Selucid Empire. The Commentary on Nahum does not refer to the Teacher at all, and there is nothing in any of the scrolls that mentions that he was ever put to death. The only allusions to his death indicate a natural death and no mention is made of the fact his followers believed him to be the Messiah. Unfortunately, the differences between fact, fiction and dramatic interpretation had not been made clear. An international team immediately declared that this had not been found in the texts.

Another scholar, A. Powell Davies, states in *The Meaning of the Dead Sea Scrolls* that the second battle is still being waged over the significance of Christian origins. He comments that the Christian church arose from a Jewish community with many of the same doctrines, sacraments and an almost identical organization. Christianity was not established through unique events, nor are the sacraments or the Gospels the original rites and word of God that Christians believe them to be. Instead of the work of God, Davies contends that Christians have derived a religion from natural social evolution.

Theologians have been bombarded with this type of reasoning and speculation on the part of scholars who give their own interpretations to their historical findings. In the past, when these interpretations differed greatly with religious dogma, the religious community's first act was to rebel and take an initiative not only against these scholars and their findings, but the importance of the scrolls, the monks of Qumran and the Essene community as well. Their efforts to justify beliefs that were challenged or in question led them to discard Christian history and to rely on their faith to determine the facts. They preferred to believe that the priesthood at Qumran and their Essene followers had no contact nor played any part in the early church, or in influencing Jesus' teachings and the Gospels.

Many of the interpretations of the scholars were in error. But the fact that organized religion has tried to discount early Christian history and play down the importance of the group that wrote the scrolls is a battle that the theologians cannot win. No matter what our Christian leaders may believe, the scrolls will not disappear. They exist and their implications are concrete. We not only have the manuscripts, but the caves, the monastery, the baptistries and the scriptorium.

The scrolls exist for what they contain and for the sign posts they provide that guide us back into the early years of the Christian faith. Although the Essene community at Qumran is gone, its words survive. Its people speak and answer questions that are as ancient as the Christian church — answers which continue to magnify and give an enlightened account of the foundations of Christianity.

11

The Gospel Writers

If the reader had the rest of the New Testament without the benefit of the Gospels, very little would be known of the life of Jesus, his attitude toward Jewish Law, his teachings of brotherly love or his other personal views. In the Gospel accounts, Jesus takes on an eminently credible personality. The words of Jesus, his parables, and the stories about him offer important features of Jewish life in the first century A.D. Other matters which are of concern are only mentioned in passing or completely taken for granted. The question is: How much history can be extracted from sources that are not primarily historical?

For centuries, the Gospels and Jesus were considered synonymous and one of the great achievements of modern scholarship is the attempt to separate Jesus and his contemporary setting from the Gospels and their literary and historical setting.[1] None of the accounts of the life of Jesus can be traced back to him directly. He did not leave any written word. What can be established about his existence came from early Christian traditions and a hypothetical written source of Jesus' teachings and sayings termed "Q" (derived from the German word "Quelle," meaning "source"), which form the basis of the Synoptic Gospels.

The Gospels represent eyewitness accounts of the life of Jesus of Nazareth but his life is outlined in a peculiar fashion. Abundant details are provided during his last three years on earth and especially his last days in Jerusalem. Little information is given about his early years, except in the accounts given by Matthew and Luke. The Gospels testify that even the witnesses to the life of Jesus were not always certain about what he had said or what he had attempted to accomplish. The reader needs to gauge the social and political situation in Galilee and Jerusalem which formed the background for his words and these events. This is gained by the study of Jewish history which tells about the life and mores of the time and about the beliefs and way of life of the priests in Qumran who were the contemporaries of John the Baptist and Jesus.

One incontestable historical fact about the life of Jesus found in other sources beside the Gospels is that he was crucified by the Romans.[2] During the eighteenth century and onwards, several historians have treated the Gospels and Christian evidence related to Jesus as pure myth. Modern archaeology and scholarship reinforced by deductions drawn from excavations in Nazareth, Jerusalem and Capernaum have proven that a man known as Jesus did exist in history. The fact that Jesus existed is not enough. Questions still loom. What was he like? How did he live? Why did he think and preach in the manner that inspired the early Christian church?

New archaeological evidence have helped to set the period of Galilee and Jerusalem during the time of the Gospels. More is known about first century Galilean religion, messianism, its manner of expression and way of life, to identify Jesus in the framework of contemporary Judaism. Drawing on this research, a flow of Jewish history from the second century B.C. through the first century A.D. can be determined.

Messianic beliefs were derived from the Jewish belief in the End of Days. The first five books of the Bible, known as the Law of Moses, requires belief in the End of Days. Therefore there exists a hope that in a time to come, the God of Israel who is master of heaven and earth will fulfill the covenant with His chosen people. Since the Jewish teaching supports a belief in a king-Messiah as well as the hope for the End of Days, the oppressed Jewish nation was open to messianic hopes.

The belief that the Messiah would walk upon the earth presaging the End of Days abounds in the apocalyptic writing of the Dead Sea Scrolls. Time and eternity would collide and human history would be absorbed into cosmic unity. These prophesies were strengthened by their learned lore in numerology, astrology, metaphysics, commentaries on history and their native symbolism.

The Jews naturally envisioned the end of the hated Roman rule and the restoration of Israel. The Pharisees discouraged these ideas, repudiated apocalyptic messianism, and adhered strictly to the text of the Bible and its approved interpretations.[3] To the Pharisees, the answer was moderation in all things. They taught that God had revealed His written Law and His oral Law. The oral Law was flexible and could be expanded, contracted, or varied by interpretation, depending on social, political and other conditions.

Members of the Dead Sea priesthood believed in the Messiahs of Aaron and Israel as prophesied by Zechariah. The priest at the End of Days would also be anointed and called "Messiah." Thus, this belief among the Dead Sea priesthood became widespread among the Jews that there would be two anointed ones, the high priest and a king of the House of David. The unique point in their literature is that the high priest assumes a greater importance than does the Messiah of the House of David. This is because the priest from the House of Zadok occupied an important position in the Dead Sea priesthood. They hoped at the End of Days to occupy Jerusalem and make one of their members high priest of the Temple.

Messianic movements and apocalyptic literature influenced Jewish religious beliefs as well as the writing of the Gospels. The Dead Sea Scrolls show that the communal meal of the Essenes was an anticipation of the Messianic Banquet.[4] An analogy of this banquet is found in the New Testament accounts of the Last Supper and the Eucharistic practices of the early Christians. Belief in a final redemption, the eschatological messiah and the Kingdom of Heaven which influenced the Gospel writers and early Christian church is based on the biblical heritage of the Jews which developed into the consequence of misfortunes for Israel.

Analysis for the source of the Gospels did not begin until the end of the seventeenth century. Students engaged in the study of the first three Gospels noted a remarkable similarity in the language at various points in the story. In 1776 a scholar named J.J. Griesbach suggested that the best means for studying the first three Gospels was to view them as a synopsis (Greek for "see together") and published the three books in parallel columns. Similarities are obvious in the wording of the books, but the patterns of agreement, character and extent become very clear when the words are aligned in columns on the same page.

Relationship between the Synoptic Gospels can be understood by using specific examples from each one in comparison with the others. Some passages reveal a close parallel between Mark and Luke with no parallel in Matthew. The significant fact is that they tell the same story while using almost identical wording. This relationship between Mark and Luke that is not shared by Matthew suggests they either used a common source or one depended directly on the other. Other selections show direct and extensive parallels between Mark and Matthew with no corresponding words in Luke. Closely worded passages between these two Gospels show a relationship not shared with Luke, or a source made available to Matthew and Mark was not available to Luke. In certain sections of the Gospels, all three share a common pattern and, at times, they use identical language. Other sections only share parallels between Matthew and Mark, or only between Luke and Mark. In some cases, all three Gospels differ — but only in a few cases do Luke and Matthew agree where Mark diverges.

The passages that are shared by Matthew and Luke but not by Mark are, with few exceptions, the sayings of Jesus. An intriguing point is that several of the identical sayings of Jesus shared by Matthew and Luke occur at radically different places. Since the relationship between Matthew and Luke relates to the sayings of Jesus, it is probable that they both made use of a source composed of the sayings of Jesus to which Mark did not have access.

Scholars agree that at least one of the Synoptic Gospels was used as a source for the other two. They base this explanation on the identity in the wording among the three books. Jesus and his followers spoke Aramaic. It is doubtful that three separate individuals could have translated random Aramaic phrases into identical Greek. Even taking into account that there may have been a tendency to harmonize the Gospels in the Greek manuscripts, most scholars believe that there was a source relationship between Matthew, Mark and Luke. They believe that Mark was the first to write his Gospel and it was shared by both Matthew and Luke independently.

All three Gospels agree in the narrative portions and follow a similar outline of Jesus' ministry. Almost all of the verses in Mark appear in Luke and Matthew, yet there is a good deal of material that is unique to Luke and Matthew. The stories that are told in Mark are in a style that was popular during the time. Matthew and Luke have each abbreviated and polished their literary versions, which makes it more likely that these alterations were made from Mark rather than Mark taking these literary versions and changing them into a longer version of a more popular form.

There are extensive parallels in Matthew and Luke which are not shared by Mark. This suggests that in addition to using Mark as a source, they also used "Q" which was made up exclusively of the teachings of Jesus. One-third of Matthew and one-fourth of Luke are derived from this source with no parallel in Mark. The various locations of many of the sayings would indicate that the source was a collection of teachings with no consecutively arranged narrative of Jesus' ministry that would tell when he gave the lesson. The identical wording makes such a source probable, though it has not been found and still remains a hypothetical entity.

Scholars theorize that Mark may have used sources which had circulated independently and were most likely oral and not written.[5] This would account for the fact that the outline of Jesus' ministry in Mark is extremely vague. Jesus spends part of his ministry in the north, proposes to travel to Jerusalem, and he travels to Jerusalem where the final drama is enacted. Mark gives little geographic detail or specificity. Instead he uses very general terms such as "one Sabbath" or "again." He sets his scenes "beside the sea" or "in the synagogue." Few episodes are related to each other. Whole incidents could be removed without affecting the narrative. The stories are tied together by Jesus' conflict with the Pharisees, his parables and miracles.

The Gospel of Mark is not a missionary work. It could not have been written to convince nonbelievers as it omits an account of Jesus' resurrection. Neither is it a biography or a work of history. The Gospel is written solely for the benefit of believers who are already familiar with the story of Jesus and have confessed him to be their messiah, rather than a work to influence potential converts.

Mark's concern over discipleship is his main reason for writing his Gospel. He instructs his readers that they must follow the proper discipleship if they are to understand Jesus. The true believer will take up his cross and dedicate his life to the service for others.

Mark warns his readers of an impending crisis — the new age will not signal the End of Days but the beginning of a time of testing. He warns that there will be opposition from Jews, dissension from within families, false prophets and messiahs who will try to lead the elect astray if they do not remain firm and alert.

The Gospel of Matthew presupposes the existence of a community of believers which is engaged in spreading the Word and in the day-to-day living of communal life.[6] The book is a practical guide to those who must serve as leaders. Some believe that Matthew composed his work as a guide for the

94

church leaders, although the work is quite different from the Manual of Discipline. It also has another purpose in addition to relating the story of Jesus and matters of Christian life.

Matthew portrays Jesus as the authorized interpreter of the Torah. He sees Jesus not as a revolutionary or innovator but as an expositor of the Law of Moses. Jesus insists that his teaching falls within a thoroughly Jewish framework which many believe makes the Gospel of Matthew the most Jewish of the four. Jesus instructs his disciples to not only preach the Law and baptize converts, but to teach their converts "to observe all that I have commanded you" (Mt. 28:20). Those who practice the teachings of Jesus are the true faithful to the Mosaic Law and the true tradition. They will enter the Kingdom of Heaven.

Luke does not present his Gospel as a disinterested historian. His objective is to firmly anchor his story in the tradition of Israel which provides legitimacy to the religious movement. Christianity is not a new religion. Its roots can be traced back to the history of the first Jew, Abraham, and even to Adam, the first man (Lk. 3:23-38). The story of Jesus belongs to the story of Israel. The events of his life fulfill God's promises made to the Jewish patriarchs through the Jewish prophets. "Everything written about me in the Law of Moses and the prophets and the psalms must be fulfilled" (Lk. 24:44).

The beginning of the Christian church is the final stage in the history of the one people of God. Luke wants to influence and convince his readers of the truth in spite of objections and opposition from the leaders of the Jewish community. The "true" Jewish community will continue to include more and more Gentiles while the gulf separating them from the Jewish community will continue to widen. Those who believe in Jesus are the legitimate heirs of the patriarchs. They are the true defenders of the Mosaic Law and the Jewish way of life. They are the New Covenant.

12

The Gospel According to John

The Fourth Gospel is in another world of thought. The vocabulary, style and content are all different. The Gospel of John includes few events recorded in the Synoptic Gospels and none of the familiar parables or aphoristic sayings. He has little to say about the practical matters of discipleship. Even the themes in his book are different. Jesus is the "Living Water," the "Bread from Heaven," the "Good Shepherd," the "True Vine," and "the Light of the World" — all images that are found nowhere else in the Synoptic Gospels. He has little to say about the practical matters of discipleship.

John's discourses are clearly related to one another. In the Synoptic Gospels, the Sermon on the Mount and Jesus' parables and sayings are frequently not integrated into the narrative. This is not true of the Fourth Gospel where it is far more difficult to isolate individual features and teachings in the story for interpretation. They are carefully constructed and usually integrated into the narratives of Jesus' miracles or signs. Even the contradictions in his writing seem to have a specific purpose.

K.G. Kuhn, a professor at the University of Göttengen, writes: "The parallels with the teaching of Jesus and the Synoptic tradition are numerous and significant. But the profound relationship with the Gospel of St. John seems to be even more important."

Millar Burrows remarks: "More than in any other part of the New Testament, contacts with the Dead Sea Scrolls have been noted by many scholars in the Gospel of John...The whole manner of thinking and literary style of John are strikingly like what we find in the Qumran texts...The similarities vary from verbal parallels to real spiritual affinity, but not to dependence or plagiarism...A style priestly and liturgical – as though the Gospel was written to be read aloud in a cathedral."

The Gospel of John could be characterized as a legal argument to be read aloud in a courtroom. Jesus is the Messiah from the beginning of his ministry and proceeds majestically through his divinely appointed program. Jesus refers to himself, his relationship to the Father, and his mission. John's carefully constructed discourses use elaborate symbolism and phrases which carry double meanings. His Gospel is a persuasion of a different view of Jesus which the Synoptic Gospels do not support, an argument aimed to move a selected group to believe that Jesus is the one who was sent to fulfill all its prophesies.

Historically, scholars could not bring the portraits of John and the Synoptics together. They have surmised that John was written probably around A.D. 120 or even as late as A.D. 150, a time when Jewish and Hellenic thought met or a time when Gnosticism[1] was at its height. The light-darkness antithesis assumes its most pronounced form in St. John's Gospel. Since this carries so much importance in John, scholars were inclined to give this Gospel a very late date.

This dualism which was popular with Gnostics has been thought to have originated in the Ancient East. The belief in a worldwide contest between the spirits of good and evil can be traced back to Zoroastrianism[2] which defines the struggle between good and evil spirits as the whole process of history. The world is devided into two camps engaged in a titanic struggle between truth and falsehood, light and darkness. The object of each force is to possess the soul of man.

Since this philosophy carries so much importance in John, scholars were inclined to give this Gospel a very late date. However, one of the scrolls contains a verse which John's Gospel nearly paraphrases, suggesting that this Gospel was written much earlier. Jewish thought and Hellenic thought had already met in the Essaeic priesthood which wrote the scrolls; Zoroastrian thought had also influenced the priests. There is no difficulty in supposing that John's Gospel was composed by an Essene or a priest of the monastery that produced the scrolls.

Under modified dualism[3] the universe is under the domain of two opposing forces. These forces are both dependent on God the Creator. Modified dualism is prevalent in both the scrolls and the New Testament. There is no predominant dualism in the Old Testament. Evil spirits exist, as the tempter in the Garden of Eden and evil men are opposed by good men, but the Old Testament does not emphasize that the world is divided into two camps locked in eternal struggle. Hebrew scriptures emphasize man's struggle to obey the Law and live righteously.

In Qumran literature, all men are aligned in one of two camps: light and truth, or darkness and perversion. Each is ruled by its own spirit or prince. While this ideology is phrased in biblical language, Zoroastrianism is clearly the inspiration of this domain; its influence on Qumran is not difficult to postulate. When the Jews were allowed to return to their homeland from Babylon, they brought with them many new ideas. Also, many Jews remained in Mesopotamia after captivity and lived side by side the Iranians. Babylonian Jews frequently traveled to Palestine. The trade routes insured continued contact among all the Jews in Diaspora. When the Qumran community came into existence, the founders had been influenced by Zoroastrian thought.

John was also influenced by modified dualism. There are traces throughout the New Testament, especially by St. Paul, but nowhere else does this dualism reach the heights or intensity it does in St. John's work. Several scholars endorse the modified dualism of St. John as influenced by the ideology and terminology of Qumran. There is enough Qumran literature to determine certain aspects of Essene thought and phrasing which may be related to the Gospel of John. Kuhn, Albright, Reiche, Brownlee, Braun and Mowry all see the Jewish background of thought and phrasing of Qumran in the Gospel, John.[4]

In 1945 the Gnostic Codices at Chenoboskion were discovered in Upper Egypt. The gap between Christianity and second century Gnosticism is tremendous. The efforts of religious historians who have tried to picture a Gnosticism which resembles the Gospel of John have been nullified. The dualism of Gnosticism is physical. The dualism of John is ethical and eschatological, like that of Qumran. Both may have had their origins in Zoroastrianism, but Gnosticism was heavily influenced by pagan Greek philosophy and Judeo-Christian heresy. Gnostic thought is a world away from that of the evangelist's work.[5]

The basis for giving John's Gospel such a late date has been eliminated. The material in John is all pre-A.D. 70 — in fact, the book that incorporates the memoirs of the Apostle John was the first of the Gospels to be written and was produced soon after the death of Jesus. The Book of John is a missionary effort directed toward the Essene community to convince them that Jesus is the Messiah. John uses familiar language to show how Christ has fulfilled all their ideals. The "Spirit of Truth" is the Holy Ghost.

Qumran has divided the world into two created camps — God loves one and He hates the other. Each camp has its own leaders or spirits. The good spirit is called the "Spirit of Truth," the "Prince of Lights," the "Angel of His Truth" and the "Holy Spirit." The evil spirit is called the "Spirit of Perversion," the "Angel of Darkness," the "Angel of Destruction." "Belial" is also a name often applied to the evil spirit. The spirits of Belial are mentioned in the Damascus Document.

The two principal spirits are personal spirits. They conduct a struggle within man by either helping or hindering him. For example: "The God of Israel and his Angel of truth have helped all the sons of light" (QS III:24-25); "And it is because of the Angel of darkness that all the sons of righteousness go astray" (QS III:21-22). "Until now the spirits of truth and perversion strive within man's heart" (QS IV:23-24). Consequently, in many instances the spirits spoken of impersonally portray man's behavior. This is not contradictory. It is natural to shift from speaking of two spirits who exercise dominion over man to speaking of two spirits of behavior in which man shows his adherence to their respective domain. *The devil* most often denotes the impersonal spirit of perversity within man that affects his negative actions.

John also uses the terms light and darkness, truth and perversion. According to John, "God is light, and in him is no darkness" (1 Jn. 1:5). With the son of God, light has come into the world. Christ is "the light of the world" (Jn. 9:5). In John, Jesus Christ replaces the Spirit of Light found in Qumran literature. He also mentions an evil spirit – the devil – but this evil spirit is the impersonal spirit that reflects on man and not the spirit leader of the forces of darkness in Qumran terminology. Neither is it the "Power of Darkness" mentioned in Luke, or "Belial" mentioned by St. Paul.

In the Qumran literature there exists a bitter struggle between two spirits until the End of Days. But for John, the struggle between light and darkness has already been decided. Christ has brought light into the world: "The darkness has not overcome the light" (Jn. 1:5). "The darkness has passed away and the true light is now shining" (1 Jn. 2:8). To John, the coming of the Christ is victorious: "But take courage, I have overcome the world" (Jn. 16:33). Christ has cast out the prince of this world. For Qumran, the victory is still somewhere in the future. For John, the light is already triumphant.

In the Qumran writings, there is the issue of predestination: "And after they exist, according to their ordinances, they fulfill their task; and nothing can be changed" (QS III:15). It would seem that man is placed under one spirit or the other and behaves accordingly. And it appears that the Sons of Light are chosen by a divine predilection independent of their works. In QS IV:22, "For God has chosen them for an eternal covenant...the ones chosen according to God's good pleasure." Such writings certainly seem to favor determinism.

On the other hand, John tries to persuade his readers that no one is determined to evil without a choice: "The light has come into the world, yet men have loved the darkness rather than the light, for their works were evil. For everyone who does evil hates the light, and does not come to the light, that his deeds may not be exposed" (Jn. 3:19-20). Christ tries to persuade men to come to the light before it is too late: "Yet a little while the light is among you. Walk while you have the light, that darkness may not overtake you. He who walks in darkness does not know where he goes" (Jn. 12:35). The idea of walking in light or darkness is similar to the ways men walk according to the Qumran texts. But with Jesus, man has a choice and can choose to walk in the light.

The Sons of Light, according to Qumran, are those who do "God's will" in a very restricted sense. One must acquaint oneself with the Torah, as explained by the Qumran community: "All who dedicate themselves to do God's ordinances shall be brought into the covenant of friendship, to be united in God's counsel...All who dedicate themselves to his truth shall bring all their mind and their strength and their property into the Community of God" (QS I:7-8). The members must accept and obey the teachings of the priesthood. The Manual of Discipline describes the Covenant of the Community. They must "walk before him perfectly in all things that are revealed according to their appointed seasons..." (QS I:8-9).

The Teacher of Righteousness was sent to them by God to instruct men in his marvelous wisdom: "And he raised them up a Teacher of Righteousness to lead them in the way of his heart" (CD I:7). It is to the Teacher of Righteousness that special wisdom was given to interpret the Torah. Acceptance of his teaching required that the member perform good works of desirable virtues which are the ways of good spirits: truth, humility, patience, compassion, understanding, wisdom, zeal and purity. Backsliding and misbehavior were seriously pun-

102

ished. In the Qumran writings, the Sons of Light are "the doers of the Law in the house of Judah whom God will deliver from the house of judgment for the sake of their labor and their faith in the Teacher of Righteousness."

As one would expect, St. John gives a different definition to the Sons of Light. It is not only good deeds that constitute a Son of Light — one must have faith in Christ and be obligated to perform good works: "Believe in the light, that you may become sons of light...I have come a light into the world, that whoever believes in me may not remain in darkness" (Jn. 12:36-46). "I am the light of the world. He who follows me does not walk in darkness, but will have the light of life" (Jn. 8:12). "He who says that he is in the light, and hates his brother, is in darkness still. He who loves his brother abides in the light, and for him there is no stumbling" (1 Jn. 2:9-10). "But if we walk in the light as he also is in the light, we have fellowship with one another, and the blood of Jesus Christ, his son, cleanse us from all sin" (1 Jn. 1:7). In this way, those who believe in Christ and keep his commandments are saved from their sins.

For Qumran, the domain of light is acceptance of the Community's interpretation of the Law. John wants the Community to accept Jesus as the long awaited Messiah. Only through Jesus Christ can one live in the light. Both John and Qumran use the modified dualistic concept of light and darkness. Both require that Sons of Light live up to their name in virtuous behavior. The terminology and ideology are the same. John wants to show the Community that Jesus is sent by the Father as the true light. St. John uses the Community's own writings to influence its thinking. He must sway them that their whole outlook in their literature and beliefs has been radically changed by the revelation that is Christ.

For Qumran, the terms "truth" and "perversity" are interchangeable with "light" and "darkness." The phraseology in John and Qumran is surprisingly similar. In QS I:5, the priests urge their followers "to practice" or "to do the truth." In Jn. 3:21, "But he who does the truth comes to the light that his deeds may be made manifest, for they have been performed in

God." In 1 Jn. 1:6, "If we say that we have fellowship with him, and walk in darkness, we die, and are not practicing the truth."

In the New Testament, "the Spirit of truth" is a term that is unique to John. In John, there is a difference between Christ and the Third Person of the Trinity, the Spirit of truth. John describes the Holy Spirit or Holy Ghost, as "the Spirit of truth," the true witness of Christ. There are three places where John mentions the Spirit of truth: "And I will ask the Father and he will give you another Advocate to dwell with you forever, the Spirit of truth whom the world cannot receive because it neither sees him nor knows him" (Jn. 14:16-17). "But when the Advocate has come, whom I will send you from the Father, the Spirit of truth who proceeds from the Father, he will bear witness concerning me" (Jn. 15:26). "But when he, the Spirit of truth has come, he will teach you all the truth" (Jn. 16:13).

The priests of Qumran are called "witnesses of truth" (QS VIII:6). Only in the Fourth Gospel, where it is used by both John the Baptist and Jesus, does this phrase occur in the New Testament: "You have sent to John, and he has borne witness to the truth" (Jn. 5:33). "I am a king. This is why I was born, and why I have come into the world, to bear witness to the truth" (Jn. 18:37). "I rejoice greatly when some brethern came and bore witness to thy truth, even as thou walkest in the truth. I have no greater joy than to hear that my children are walking in the truth" (3 Jn. 3).

Both in John and in Qumran literature, truth is a means of purification and sanctification. QS IV:20-21 states, "And then God will purge by his truth all the deeds of man...to cleanse him through the Holy Spirit from all wicked practices, sprinkling upon him a Spirit of truth as purifying water." Jn. 17:17-19 says to, "Sanctify them in truth. Thy word is truth. Even as thou hast sent me into thy world, so I also have sent them into the world. And for them I sanctify myself, that they also may be sanctified in truth."

Qumran literature maintains that one must love good and

104

hate evil. The individual is admonished to separate himself from perverse men, and to conceal from them the true meaning of the Law (QS V; IX). In QS I:3-4: "To love everything that He has chosen, and to hate everything that He has rejected; to keep afar from every evil and to cling to every good deed." And in QS I:10 it is required, "To hate all the sons of darkness each according to his guilt in provoking God's vengeance!" Also in QS IV:24, "According as man's inheritance is in truth and righteousness, so he hates evil; but insofar as his heritage is in the portion of perversity and wickedness in him, so he abominates truth."

The Manual of Discipline commands that there be a spirit of loving devotion in the Community: "To love all the sons of light, each according to his lot in God's counsel" (QS I:10). "One shall not speak to his brother in anger, or in complaint, or with a stiff neck or a callous heart, or a wicked spirit; nor shall he hate him..."

The Synoptic Gospels state Christ's command for brotherly love. But it is John who stresses love of one's brother outside the Community. Christ's greatest commandment is that of mutual love: "A new commandment I give you, that you love one another: that as I have loved you, you also love one another. By this will all men know that you are my disciples, if you have love for one another" (Jn. 13:34-35; Jn. 15:12). "He who loves his brother abides in the light, and for him there is no stumbling" (1 Jn. 2:10). John's emphasis is: "Beloved, let us love one another, for love is from God...He who does not love does not know God, for God is love" (1 Jn. 4:7-8).

"Fountain of living waters" is a metaphorical term used in the Damascus Document. A direct reference is made in CD IX:28 to the Hasidim who left the Community and returned to Jerusalem to become Pharisees: "...all the men who entered into the New Covenant in the Land of Damascus and yet turned backward and acted treacherously and departed from the spring of living waters..." the Community's interpretation of the Law being the "spring of living waters." And for those who stayed in the Land of Damascus: "They digged a well of many waters:

and he that despises them shall not live" (CD V:13). "The well is the Law, and they who digged it are the penitents of Israel who went forth out of the land of Judah and sojourned in the Land of Damascus" (CD VIII:6).

This terminology occurs in only two places in the New Testament — in the Fourth Gospel and in John's Revelation. When Christ speaks to the Samaritan woman he says: "He, however, who drinks of the water that I will give him shall never thirst; but the water that I will give him shall become in him a fountain of water, springing up into life everlasting" (Jn. 4:14). Also in Jn. 7:38, "He who believes in me, as the Scripture says, 'From within him there shall flow rivers of living water.' " In Revelation 21:6, Christ, who is the Alpha and Omega, promises: "To him who thirsts I will give of the fountain of the water of life freely."

John uses other Essaeic ideologies in his continuous persuasion that the Old Testament prophesies are fulfilled through Christ, just as he does with the concept of modified dualism. His ideas of truth and perversity and "the Spirit of truth" run parallel to Qumran writings with steadfast consistency. John stresses brotherly love, and his use of the term "fountain of living waters," although quite familiar in the scrolls, is not found in the Synoptic Gospels. According to John, one can only accept the Law through the interpretation of Christ. For John, "*your* Law," the Law of the Essene Priesthood, is no longer "*our* Law."[6]

Scholars once believed that Mark, being the earliest written of the Gospels and the source for Matthew and Luke, was a closer avenue to the historical Jesus and the events of his life. But since John predates the other Gospels, this document is now considered to be the most historically accurate. Archaeology tends to support this theory. Where the Fourth Gospel differs from the others, modern scholars such as C.H. Dodd[7] and R.T. Fortna[8] credit John with greater historical credence.

John treats the material he shares with the Synoptics, in a different manner.[9] Jesus' public ministry lasts three years and begins with a baptizing ministry in the Jordan Valley.

Jesus makes frequent journeys to Jerusalem where he clashes with the authorities over a long period of time. There is a Roman connivance in Jesus' arrest and complicity on the part of Caiaphas, the Jewish high priest, in the trial of Jesus. Finally, the death of Jesus occurs on Passover eve, not on Passover day.

John's account in these respects is more accurate than the Synoptic account. According to Raymon E. Brown, Jesus had a baptizing ministry before he began his teaching ministry. His public ministry lasted more than one year. He traveled to Jerusalem many times and his opposition to Jewish authorities in Jerusalem was not limited to his last days. Old Testament speculation about the personified wisdom of John, along with thought patterns of Essaeic Judaism at Qumran, go a long way to fill in the background of Johannine vocabulary and expressions.

The author of the Fourth Gospel is also believed to be the writer of the three Epistles of John.[10] It is also believed that John, the "disciple whom Jesus loved," was one of the 12 Apostles. John's writing uses language familiar to the priests of Qumran and the Community. It is intended to show how Christ fulfilled all their ideas. He is the light of which they speak. The Spirit of truth is the Holy Ghost. The true Sons of Light are those who believe in Jesus Christ.

It has always been known that Christianity emerged out of Judaism. But for modern man, his unconscious thought has been to view Christianity as a new religion. Where the Gospels view Jesus as fulfilling the prophecies of the patriarchs, modern man tends to see him as the founder of a new religion. Jesus is the inventor of Christianity, the founder of his church and guardian of his new ideas. In his church there is something new, something never heard of before. For the Gospels, this view is diametrically opposed. They emphasize that all is "old." The golden rule is not a new idea or ethical achievement of a new moral thinker; it is recommended by his remark, "This is the Law and the Prophets."

The issue between the monks of Qumran and the early

Christians was not one of originality. They contested the question of who were the legitimate heirs of God's covenant, the prophetic promises, and who could provide the most striking arguments for fulfillment. The word "Christianity" was not coined in the Gospels. There was no need for such an abstraction. The Gospels spoke of the good news, promises that had been fulfilled, and members of their church as the true people of God. These were the chosen ones who had accepted Jesus' messianic claims and his church.

Modern man has never confronted what John the Baptist, Jesus, and the Church of Jesus may have inherited from the Essenes. He will not face these questions as long as he devotes himself to his own pattern of thought. But the early Christian church did not depend on its originality. In the time when the church emerged from Judaism, originality was never an issue. Christianity emerged as a church and a community, not as a new thought system.

The scrolls enhance the background of Christianity. They add so much that the significance of similarities rescues Christianity from claims of originality in the modern sense and leads back to the true foundation of the church by way of the person who was Jesus and the events of the Messiah.

13

The Messianic Age

So the fullness of time came. The greatest event of all ages was about to unfold. Of the 5 million Jews in the world at the time, by far the greater number lived outside of Palestine in the Diaspora.[1] Many Jews who lived in the world dominated by pagan culture, compromised and lost their traditional Mosaic faith. The faithful maintained their heritage through the ever-present synagogue. Of the 1.5 million inhabitants in Palestine, about a third were Jews. The Jews were mostly concentrated in the southern province of Judea. Along with the Jews were communities of Greeks and Samaritans. Palestine was controlled by Rome and ruled by Herod the Great, their own appointee.

The Samaritans occupied the territory surrounding the city of Samaria, an area that laid directly between Galilee to the north and Judea to the south. There was so much hostility between Jews and Samaritans that the traveling Jew often journeyed the more circuitous route around Samaria, east of the Jordan valley through Perea. Samaritans were descendants of the Northern Kingdom. The Assyrians had conquered Samaria, their capital, in 721 B.C. and carried off their most capable citizens. Those who remained behind intermarried with local pagans and foreigners who drifted into the land.

When members of the Southern Kingdom returned from exile, Samaria's people were a mixed race with a corrupted form of religion. Jews despised Samaritans nearly as much as they despised Gentiles and pagans.

Not only did the Jews have to contend with Samaritans, but Gentiles inhabited all of Palestine. Palestine, as well as the entire Mediterranean area, spoke Greek, thought Greek, and was molded in many ways as a single cultural community. Greek culture had its affect not only on Jews in Diaspora but on those in Palestine as well. There had been forced attempts to Hellenize the Judeans in Palestine. Hellenization had gone a long way and Jerusalem had already become very much a Greek city before the Maccabean revolt. The rebellion interrupted this movement, but it had already become and remained a bitter national and religious issue.

When the Romans marched into Jerusalem, the Greek influence continued unabated. This meant that Greek esthetics, Greek physical culture, Greek ethics, and Greek paganism had all penetrated Jerusalem and the Jewish way of life. At the turn of Eras, Jerusalem was, for all practical purposes as were many other Palestinian cities, completely Hellenized. Travel throughout the country was impossible without touching or tasting the culture of the Roman Empire. Jerusalem was engulfed in the very cosmopolitan atmosphere of Greek daily living, dress, thought, entertainment, sports, customs, culture and paganism.

Various Jewish sects modeled themselves after philosophical schools prevalent in Greco-Roman society.[2] Literary forms, advice of rabbinic sages, tradition and the pattern of rabbinic Judaism were all influenced by the Greco-Roman phenomena. Even the rules established by the rabbinic authorities for interpreting the Jewish Bible were derived from Greek principles of interpretation.

Among the 500,000 Jews living in Palestine during the first century B.C., only about 6,000 male adults were Pharisees.[3] The group that separated from the True Remnant at Qumran was more moderate in its interpretation of the Law of

110

Moses. The group's power was in its control of the Temple. Religious zeal required obedience to the oral and the written Law and practices were founded on the Law of Moses. However, the oral tradition of their great teachers was highly emphasized and this contributed to a sizeable group of laws developed to govern man's daily behavior. These oral laws were flexible to allow for changes in the contemporary and social climate.

Pharisees discouraged belief in the End of Days and a king-Messiah who would come and turn the world order upside down. Their power lay in their control of the Temple and they had no interest in political events. They saw no need for a religious upheaval to return them to the Temple — the high priest was a Pharisee. Their interest was in moderation and tolerance within the Hellenized world of the Romans.

Socially, there was quite a division between the peoples of Palestine during the first century B.C. Not only was there a sharp distinction between Jews and Gentiles, there was also a harsh distinction between the religious and nonreligious. Men and women did not share equal stature. There was disagreement on how much one should bow to Rome. But probably the most pronounced contrasts were apparent in the economic distinctions between the wealthy and the very poor.

The aristocracy in Palestine used its great wealth and economic power to control religion. Members of the upper class were religious. They despised the poor who could not afford to observe the religious law to the minute detail. The Pharisees and Sadducees epitomized the religious elite, but these accounted for only a small percentage of the population, the rest of the people were poor.

The people of the land not only suffered under Roman taxation and cruelty but they were also subjected to the haughty disdain of their own religious leaders. They could not be trusted with secrets. Their testimony was unworthy in a court of law. The poor could not be appointed as guardian of an orphan. Intermarriage was absolutely forbidden between the aristocracy and the poor. Some of the Jews were so poor they became slaves, a practice permitted by Jewish Law.[4]

The people of the Essene community were "the Poor of God," "the Poor in Spirit." The priests at Qumran and their followers were reknown for their kindness, their equality, their indifference to money, worldly achievements and pleasures. They were only interested in what was truly important in life — piety, holiness, justice, as well as the love of God, virtue and of man. They had the knowledge of what was truly good, evil and of what was indifferent. They lived throughout small villages and colonies where their communal living required a common storehouse, common vestments, and a common treasury where they placed all their earnings and from which expenditures were made on the behalf of all.

The Essaeic movement was widely spread, not only through Judea but also in Diaspora. It consisted of a large number of communities linked by their beliefs and practices into what may be called a "church."[5] It is clear that this church was not associated with the synagogues of the Pharisees but maintained synagogues of its own. Although there may have been some asceticism on the part of the priests at Qumran, nowhere in their writings is their any indication that the Essene community was monastic. Philo said, "The Essenes inhabited many cities of Judea, as well as many villages and populous tracts...their membership in the sect is from freedom of choice and not as a matter of race."

The priests of the monastery were expert astronomers and astrologers. The Jewish priesthood had learned astronomy during exile in Babylon. The movements of the stars were used to predict future events. The time for the coming of the Messiah was recorded, as was a horoscope for the blessed event. Josephus writes: "...they foretell of things to come...and it is seldom they miss in their predictions."

From Cave IV, known as the Partridge Cave, came the Scrolls of the Horoscopes. Included was the Horoscope of the Messiah, translation by G. Vermes. In Horoscopes (186:2):

"His eyes are black and glowing. His beard is red. His

voice is gentle. His teeth are fine and well aligned. He is neither tall nor short. And his fingers are thin and long. And his thighs are smooth. And his toes are well aligned. His spirit consists of eight parts in the House of Light and one part in the House of Darkness. And this is his birthday on which he is to be born...

"And his hair will be red. And there will be lentils on...and small birthmarks on his thigh. And after two years he will know how to distinguish one thing from another. In his youth, he shall be like a man who knows nothing until the time when he knows the three Books.

"And then he will acquire wisdom and learn understanding...vision to come to him on his knees. And with his father and his ancestors... life and old age. Counsel and prudence will be with him, and he will know the secrets of man. His wisdom will reach all the people, and he will know the secrets of all the living. And all their designs against him will come to nothing, and his rule over all the living will be great. His designs will succeed for he is the Elect of God. His birth and the breath of his spirit...and his designs shall be forever..."

An account of the birth of Jesus, his early years, and his ministry on earth is given in the Gospels. However, much information about Jesus is lacking either because the writers thought it was not required or because they assumed that the reader would have a good background knowledge already. The scrolls offer a wealth of information to be drawn upon in explaining the Gospel passages and filling in Gospel background. Of course, as in any issue, there are an infinite number of possible explanations. But by drawing from this new valuable source of background material, one can fill in the thoughts of the Gospel writers and answer questions with the only logical answers.

No mention is made in the Gospels of a movement under the name of "Christians" or "Christianity." The name "Christian" was not used by those who would be later known by this name. Instead, people who were involved in the movement that would eventually acquire this name called themselves "the Saints," "the Brethren," "the Chosen," "the Elect," "they that are of the Lord," "they that Believe," "the Sons of Light," "the Disciples," "the Poor," "they that are of the Way," "the New Covenant," and other similar appellations.

It may also be noted that those to whom the name "Essene" refers did not call themselves by that name. The name neither appears in any of the discovered documents nor in any of the books that may be termed "Essaeic," the Gospels or the New Testament. The Essenes used the same names to apply to themselves in their own writings as those used by the early Christians.

"Essene" was first penned by Josephus in The Jewish War. Many possible explanations of this Greek word have been advanced. Josephus says that these people collected therapeutic herbs and minerals, and that they were skilled in the art of healing. The Aramaic word for "healer" or "physician," is "asya," (plural "asayya") and is very close to the Greek word for "Essene," "Essaioi" (plural "Essenoi"). The Aramaic word for "myrtle," which was famed in antiquity for its medicinal properties, is "asa" (plural "asayya"), which is almost the same as the Aramaic word for "healer."

In the Book of Zechariah, he writes that the "myrtles" which stood in Mesillah were interpreted homiletically as the "pious ones," a title claimed by the Essenes for themselves. The idea of a place of healing near the Dead Sea in Jewish tradition gives one added reason for the Essenes ("Physicians") choice of Qumran (Messillah) as their desert home. The fact that the brotherhood in Alexandria, which had much in common with those at Qumran, called itself "the Therapeutae" leads one to believe that this is the correct derivation of "Essene."[6]

The Gospels Mark and John contain no record of Jesus' life prior to his ministry. The description given by Matthew and Luke are quite different. They both recount that Jesus was born in Bethlehem of a young virgin woman.

Luke describes Elizabeth and Zechariah, the parents of

John the Baptist, as blessed with a pregnancy. Luke relates that when Elizabeth was six months pregnant, her babe leaped in her womb at the appearance of Mary who was newly pregnant. Elizabeth also recognized Mary as having the blessed one in her womb. Zechariah is described as a priest of the Pharisees and his wife is also of priestly lineage. Luke says that John's parents are "righteous before God, walking in all the commandments and ordinances of the Lord blameless."

Joseph and Mary are described as zealous Jews — even more so than a temple priest and his wife who are righteous before God, and who obey all His commandments and ordinances. This could only be possible if Mary and Joseph were members of the Essene community, for no other group saw themselves as being more pious than the Pharisees. In their Messianic Anthology, the priests of Qumran believed the Messiah would arise from within the Community — Jesus fulfilled this belief.[7]

Zechariah did his work as a priest before God, taking his turn in the daily service. The angel Gabriel appeared and told him that he was chosen to have a son, strong and mighty, like the prophet Elijah. His son would prepare the Lord's people. When Zechariah doubted the message of Gabriel, he was struck dumb and remained so until the promise was fulfilled.

When Zechariah came out of the Temple the people recognized that he had seen a vision. Since he was unable to talk, he made signs with his hands. When John was born, Zechariah regained his speech and he praised the Lord. Neighbors who witnessed this were filled with fear and the story spread throughout Judea.

Zechariah raised up a psalm — an eschatological prophecy — about the king-Messiah, the son of David, who was to come: he would save Israel from her enemies and from the power of those who hate. He would come to fulfill the covenant. Zechariah's son, John, would become a prophet who would go ahead of the Lord to prepare his road for him.

To the Pharisees, Zechariah was an embarrassment and a threat. Not only did he lend support to the eschatological beliefs of the Essenes, he gave an eye witness account and was a bearer of news from the angel Gabriel. Even his son was to take an active part in the events that would bring about the End of Days.

In Lk. 11:49-51 Jesus refers to John's father, Zechariah, who was murdered by the Pharisees because he was a witness and messenger to the Messianic story. Jesus gives the exact location where Zechariah was killed when he confronts the Pharisees and chastises them: "...I will send them prophets and messengers, some of whom they will kill and persecute...from the blood of Abel to the blood of Zechariah, who was killed between the altar and the holy place."

Luke also reports that Caesar Augustus sent out a decree that a census should be taken; and that all the world should be taxed. This taxing was made when Cyrenius was governor of Syria. "Cyrenius the governor" was the same Senator P. Sulpicius Quirinius, known from existing Roman documents. Quirinius was sent by Emperor Augustus to Syria during the reign of Saturninus, the pro-counsel. Quirinius established his seat in Syria between 10 B.C. and 7 B.C. All citizens went to be taxed into their own cities. Joseph and Mary left for Bethlehem, because Joseph was of the lineage of King David.

Mary gave birth to Jesus in Bethlehem. On the eighth day he was circumcised, according to custom. After about one month, fulfilling the required days of purification, Mary and Joseph took Jesus to the Temple in Jerusalem to dedicate their child and to offer the prescribed Levitical sacrifice. Either a lamb or a dove would be acceptable, depending on their economic circumstances. Mary and Joseph took a dove, evidence of their poverty.

Sometime later, after Mary and Joseph returned to Bethlehem, the Magi came to pay homage. "Magi" does not mean "wise men," but taken in the context, is closer to meaning "astrologers." Matthew does not say they are three in number, nor are they kings. He does make mention of a rising star, a reference to a messianic prophecy in Numbers 24:17, "A star shall come forth out of Jacob, and a scepter shall rise out of

Israel." In Mt. 2:1-2, "Jesus was born in the town of Bethlehem, in the land of Judea, during the time when Herod was king. Soon afterwards some men who studied the stars came from the east to Jerusalem and asked: 'Where is the baby born to be king of the Jews? We saw his star when it came up in the east, and we have come to worship him'."

The Messianic Star has stimulated man's imagination for ages. For laymen and experts alike, just about every possible explanation has been offered for anything that has ever moved across the heavens. The Bible describes in very specific terms a quite unusual event and one would expect modern astronomers to have a scientific explanation.

One night, just before Christmas in 1603, the Imperial Mathematician and Astronomer Royal Johannes Kepler was working in Prague while studying the approach of two planets. The technical term for two celestial bodies on the same degree of longitude is a "conjunction." Kepler remembered reading the notes of Abarbanel, a rabbinic writer, which referred to the special significance of a particular conjunction of planets. The Messiah would appear when Saturn and Jupiter came together in the constellation of Pisces.

Kepler wondered if this announced the real coming of the "Star of Bethlehem," or perhaps this constellation was the "Christmas Star." He made the calculations for a conjunction about the time of the birth of Christ and checked his calculations again and again. The result was a threefold conjunction within the space of a year! His astronomical calculations gave the year as 7 B.C.

In 1925, German scholar P. Schnabel discovered some ancient neo-Babylonian cuneiform papers of the School of Astrology at Sippar, in Babylonia. He found a note recorded among the series of dates and observations on the position of the planets in the constellation of Pisces. Jupiter and Saturn had been tracked during a period of five months — the calendar year was 7 B.C.!

Modern astronomers can turn back the cosmic clock in planetariums by simply rearranging the skies as they appeared thousands of years ago for any given year, month or even a day. The position of the planets can be calculated with precision. Astronomers have discovered just as did Kepler, that Jupiter and Saturn had met in Pisces during the year 7 B.C. — and they had met three times. These three conjunctions had been clearly visible in the Mediterranean area. The first conjunction occurred on May 29th, visible for two hours in the morning sky; the second conjunction took place on October 3rd; and the last took placed on December 4th. By the end of January in 6 B.C., Jupiter had moved from Pisces into the constellation of Aries.

Matthew writes, "We have seen his star in the east." This translation however is not correct. In the Greek version, "in the east" is written "En té anatolé" — the Greek singular. Elsewhere "the east" is written "anatolai" — the Greek plural. The singular form, "anatolé," has an astronomical significance: it implies the observation of the early rising of a star, the heliacal rising. The translators of the authorized version of the Bible didn't know this. When "en té anatolé" is properly translated, Matthew 2:2 reads: "We have seen his star appear in the first rays of dawn." This translation corresponds exactly with the astronomical facts.[8]

The coming of the Messiah had been predetermined. During the Exile, the Jewish priests in Babylon had learned and studied astronomy at the school in Sippar. The priests who returned to Israel from Babylon had the knowledge to forecast such a conjunction of Saturn and Jupiter. They took this knowledge with them when they left Jerusalem and went into the desert. They made their calculations and wrote their horoscopes. The writings were made known to their Essene brothers in Syria and Egypt. The priesthood in Diaspora would also be able to read the skies and recognize this sign. It was a delegation from the Essene brotherhood, either from Egypt or Syria (or perhaps both), that traveled to Bethlehem to see the newly born King of the Jews.

Matthew writes that when the Magi arrived in Israel, they visited King Herod and when he heard the news he became

118

very troubled. Matthew tells his readers that Herod ordered the slaughter of innocent children in an attempt to murder the king-Messiah. Although this cruel deed could fit perfectly within the realm of Herod's wicked personality, history does not record that this order actually occurred. The Magi had the prophecies of the Messiah and knew he was born in Bethlehem. They must have known the possible danger they would create by alerting Herod to a possible threat to his throne.

Matthew may have used this story to draw a parallel between the birth of Jesus and that of Moses and to show how certain prophecies had been fulfilled. Just as Moses, Jesus had been miraculously delivered from the hand of a wicked king who had decreed the death of all male children. It also made the saying of the prophet Jeremiah come true: "A sound is heard in Ramah, the sound of bitter crying and weeping. Rachel weeps for her children, she weeps and will not be comforted, because they are all dead." Jesus is the new Moses. But Matthew does not develop this theme. He is more interested in Christ as the Messiah; but there are other allusions to the Mosaic image in Matthew — such as Jesus providing an extended exposition of God's will from a mountain.[9]

The Essene brotherhood began numbering the years in the new era with Jesus' seventh birthday. Age 7 was known as the "age of reason" in the Ancient East. It was believed that this was when one could first distinguish right from wrong. This numbering of years in the name of Jesus was later continued by the early Christian church.

One other account is made of Jesus' early life. When Jesus was 12 he accompanied Joseph and Mary to the Passover feast in Jerusalem for his bar mitzvah, which marked his becoming a responsible member in the Jewish community. For the first time it is disclosed that Jesus was aware of his very important mission as the Messiah. From the time of the Nativity to his association with John the Baptist, nothing more is told of Jesus other than this solitary account at the age of 12 when he visited the Temple.

Historically we have no information as to how he hap-

119

pened to come to possess unprecedented spiritual and moral insight. One can surmise about these "years of silence" based on knowledge of Jewish families, educational, social, economic and religious customs. But who can fathom the birth and growth of the genius type in ancient Palestine?

Jesus' early years are veiled from history. The writers of the Gospel were not concerned about this phase of his life because, in retrospect, it was not important. The Gospels begin where Jesus' life became theologically meaningful. They give an account of a worker-of-wonders who taught and performed cures in Galilee and died in Jerusalem. Much has been written on the early life of Jesus using speculations and theories, and sometimes using modern historic criteria. Most of these works completely ignore the Essene movement. The archaeological discovery of the scrolls throws considerable light on the Community's lifestyle during Jesus' early years. Jesus was raised in an Essene community and was subjected to the Community's requirements for young adult men.

Many scholars believe that Jesus had early contact with the Qumran priesthood because of his knowledge of their doctrine and he often had them in mind when he taught. It has even been conjectured that Jesus lived for some years among the Qumran priests.

In the Manual of Discipline and the Damascus Document, specific instruction is given about worshiping on the correct days of the calendar:

"They shall not depart from any command of God concerning their times; they shall be neither early nor late for any of their appointed times..."

"They shall keep the Sabbath day according to its exact interpretation, and the feasts and the Day of Fasting according to the finding of the members of the New Covenant in the Land of Damascus...and as for the exact statement of their periods to put Israel in remembrance in regard to all these, behold, it is treated accurately in the Book of the Divisions of

120

the Seasons according to their Jubilees and their Weeks."

For the priests at Qumran, their whole life was one of uninterrupted worship. The Manual of Discipline, however, required that they worship God in the correct manner and at set times. These set times were eternal and unchanging, conforming to the rhythm of time itself. Most Jews followed the Hellenistic lunar calendar which effected a compromise between the lunar year (354 days) and the solar seasons of solstice and equinox. Following three years of 36 months, this calendar inserted one supplementary month.

In opposition to the Gentile calendar, the Book of Jubilees presented a solar calendar which God announced to Moses.[10] It is this calendar attested to by Jubilees and Enoch that the Manual of Discipline refers. This solar calendar is based on "the laws of the Great Light of Heaven," in which the year is divided into exactly 52 weeks. Each season consists of three months with 30 days and each season is connected by one day to the next season.

This solar calendar recommended itself to the Community for its belief in God's unchanging order in the universe. Each year always begins on Wednesday, the fourth day in the Jewish week. This conforms perfectly with the work of God who created the sun on the fourth day. Not only does the year begin on Wednesday, but so does every season. Any date always falls on the same day in every year. Passover, the 15th day of the first month, always falls on Wednesday, whereas the Day of Atonement, the 10th day of the seventh month, always occurrs on Friday. This calendar caused the Essenes to celebrate the feast days on separate days from the rest of Judaism.[11]

An essential part of the Law of Moses holds that worship is only valid in the Temple of Jerusalem. But the priests at Qumran regarded the Temple priests as celebrating on all the wrong days,[12] their officiating as wicked, the Temple profaned by uncleanness and the orthodox liturgical calendar unlawful. In Hymn 19 of the Psalms Scroll, the Community proclaims that observance of the Gentile calendar is an abomination and directly counter to the "certain Law from the mouth of God."

The Community faced this dilemma in the following way: despite the wicked practices of the Temple priesthood, sacrificial worship was not condemned. The Community's priests and Levites were forbidden to take an active part in performing Temple services. The Damascus Document VI states that the priests could send their offerings to the Temple, provided they were carried by a person in a state of ritual purity and not placed on the alter on a Sabbath day (CD XI). At the End of Days, which followed the Community's conquest of Jerusalem, the Temple would be reorganized according to the Essene statues. This was scheduled to take place in the seventh year of the final 40 years' war of the Sons of Light against the Sons of Darkness (QM II).

Meanwhile, the Council of the Community fulfilled the role of the sanctuary.[13] Essene families traveled to Qumran to celebrate their religious observances. They set up their tents on the marl terrace and stayed in the nearby caves. They paid their taxes to the priests as evidenced by the jars of coins that were found buried in the ruins. On Passover, and for special dedications, the Community members were also required by the Law to travel to the Temple in Jerusalem to observe their religious holidays. There they also fulfilled their worship, made offerings and paid the Temple tax.

Young Jesus traveled to Qumran with his family many times and the priests there knew that he was the one born to fulfill the Messianic prophecies. Nevertheless, women and children had no place or status in the Community's structured worship services. Contact with women or children by the priesthood was forbidden. Only when Jesus attained the required age would he be eligible to begin training to become an adult member of the Essene community. According to the Messianic Rule I, initiation to enter the Community would begin on his twentieth birthday: "At the age of 20 years he shall be enrolled, that he may enter upon his allotted duties in the midst of his family and be joined to the holy congregation."

Following this two-year initiation process, he must serve in the Community until age 25 when he then becomes a junior member: "At the age of 25 years he may take his place among the foundations [the lower ranks] of the holy congregation to work in the service of the congregation."

It is not until the age of 30 that full and senior member status is achieved to be among the leaders of the Community: "At the age of 30 years he may approach to participate in lawsuits and judgments, and may take his place among the chiefs of the Thousands of Israel, the chiefs of the Hundreds, Fifties, and Tens, the Judges and the officers of their tribes, in all their families under the authority of the sons of Aaron the Priests (MR, I)."

John the Baptist, his disciples, and the Essene community were not familiar with Jesus when he appeared to be baptized at the Jordan River. Although they recognized him as a Nazarene, the son of Mary and Joseph the carpenter, they still did not know him. John the Baptist states: "After me comes a man who ranks before me, for he was before me. I myself did not know him; but for this I come baptizing with water, that he might be revealed to Israel. I myself did not know him; but he who sent me to baptize with water said to me, 'He on whom you see the Spirit descend and remain, this is he who baptizes with the Holy Spirit' " (Jn. 1:30-33).

If Jesus had begun his training at Qumran at the age of 20, the entire Community would have already been well familiar with him upon his appearance at the Jordan River. But this was not the case. The only explanation is that Jesus studied with an Essene priesthood outside of Palestine. This required that he depart his homeland prior to his twentieth year.

The most likely place for Jesus to have begun his initiation into the Community was with the Essene brotherhood in Alexandria. There the Theraputae, known as the "Contemplative Essenes," lived their religious lives by the same rigid tenets and strict discipline as did the Essene priests in Israel. If this had been the home of the Magi, what a letter of introduction for Jesus to journey there with the gifts they had presented him at his birth! Jesus began his initiation into the Essene community and completed his studies at the age of 30.

Moses, Elijah, or some other member of the prophetic line was expected to precede the Messiah to prepare the way for him. This pattern of thought was continued by the Christian church to explain the relationship of John the Baptist to their Messiah, Jesus Christ. The Baptist was initiated into the Essene community at Qumran. John was familiar with Essene thoughts regarding the coming of the Messianic Age. He may even have been reared by the Community at Qumran (probably at 'Ain Feshkha). Luke represents John as having gone into the wilderness as a mere boy. The historian Josephus in his description of the Essene priests says, "Marriage they disdain, but adopt other men's children, while yet pliable and docile, and regard them as their kin and mold them in accordance with their own principles."

Brownlee and Schubert both suggest that John may have been one of these adoptions.[14] No one else lived in the Judean desert who could care for John and give him the proper training for his prophetic mission. With the death of Zechariah at the hands of the Pharisees in the Temple, there was as much danger to John. The only safe action would have been for his mother to seek the safety and refuge of the Qumran community for it alone could protect him from the Pharisees.

John was taken and reared by the priests at Qumran following the death of his father. This life with the Community fills a very important blank in the life of John the Baptist and explains in a marvelous way the teachings of John. For those skeptical of the nativity story, this allows for the embodying of true historical traditions, such as the fact that John was born to very old parents and that he grew up in the desert.

The Baptist is a very graphic character. He was clothed with camel's hair and had a leather girdle around his waist. He ate locust and wild honey. John's ministry is in the wilderness of Judea, defined in the Old Testament as the stretch of desolate hills along the west bank of the Dead Sea. The scrolls

124

record that the dress of the members of the Community was identical to John's and they shared the same diet. The desert on the west bank of the Dead Sea is precisely the location of Qumran. All four Gospels record that John was fulfilling the prophecy of Isaiah: "I am the voice of one crying in the wilderness, 'Make straight the way of the Lord,' as the prophet Isaiah said" (Jn. 1:23).

The Manual of Discipline explains why the Community was in the desert: "They will separate themselves from the midst of the habitation of perverse men to go to the wilderness to clear the way of the Lord, as it is written: 'In the wilderness clear the way of the Lord; level in the desert a highway for our God.' So as to do according to all that was revealed time after time according to that which the prophets revealed through His Holy Spirit" (QS VIII:13-16).

This clearing of the way for the Lord was in preparation for the Messianic Age. If they were good enough, God would honor them by sending the Messiah who, just as Moses had appeared in the wilderness, would also appear and lead his people into the Promised Land of the Messianic Kingdom.[15] This stretch of wilderness was chosen because, in Isa. 40:3, the words for "wilderness" designated the basin of the Dead Sea. This was where the Lord's glory would be revealed in the work of the Messiah. Their study and practice of the Law would bring about this day.

John had particular importance to the priests of Qumran. Beside the fact that from the time of his birth it was known he was born to take an active part in the Messianic prophecies, John was also of the lineage of a priest. He entered the training and initiation at the age of 20 and completed 10 years of training at Qumran as a full priest of the Community and prepared to complete his mission at the age of 30.

The Baptist left Qumran and traveled to the ford at the Jordan River, a mere six miles from the Qumran monastery, and there he began to prepare for the magnificent events to come. John, being born six months before Jesus, accomplished his studies almost concurrently with Jesus in Alexandria. John

125

and the priests at Qumran knew that six months after John completed his training Jesus would complete his required training and preparation for his heavenly ministry. John baptized, preached repentance and called for the Messiah to come forth. This then fulfilled what the Lord had spoken by the prophet, "Out of Egypt have I called my son."

Based on Kepler's calculations marking the birth of Jesus in the year 7 B.C., he began his ministry in A.D. 23: "in the fifteenth year of the reign of Tiberius Caesar, Pontius Pilate being governor of Judea, and Herod being tetrarch of Galilee, and his brother Philip tetrarch of the region of Iturae'a and Trachonitis and Lysanias tetrarch of Abilene, in the high-priesthood of Annas and Caiaphas" (Lk. 3:1-2).

John the Baptist became the first outside spokesman for the priesthood of Qumran.[16] His preaching was based on the coming of the Day of Judgment and the advent of the coming Messiah. The word flew round Judea and Galilee of a new prophet that had arisen. The long silence had been broken by the powerful personality that the Fourth Gospel portrays as the "Essene Baptist."

According to the Fourth Gospel, the Baptist denies being either the prophet Elijah, or the Messiah. He is the "voice" referred to in Isaiah 40:3. In this Gospel it appears that the Baptist is demoted from being Elijah to "a voice crying in the wilderness."

For the Synoptic Gospels, John the Baptist is assumed to be Elijah by the words of Jesus himself. During the time the Synoptics were written there was a strong rivalry between the Christian and Essene movements. It was wiser not to demote the Baptist but move him instead to as high a position as possible — to that of Christ. To use the Baptist as Elijah would inject a note of conciliation. No one would have attributed a speech to the Baptist which contradicts Jesus proclaiming the Baptist as Elijah; but this is the case in the Fourth Gospel. St. John wrote his Gospel sufficiently before the Synoptics not to know of their writings.

126

The Baptist preached Essene thoughts of the coming Messianic Age. He believed that "the way" was to be prepared in the wilderness where the Messiah would make his appearance (Jn. 1:33). John required penitents to perform acts of mercy and avoid evil. His moral requirements are confirmed by Josephus: "He ordered the Jews to perform acts of mercy, to do what was right to their neighbors, and worship God in all sincerity and be eligible for repentance and baptism" (Antiq. XVIII:17).

John the Baptist also believed the Jewish nation was apostate and sinful. Jews could not become the people of God unless they repented, changed their way of life and were baptized. John's baptism, like that of the Essenes', was not an institutionalized discipline without moral bearing. Baptism could only cleanse man of his sins if it was preceded by his repentance.[17]

According to the Baptist, entry into the Covenant of God is not a stipulated birthright — being born a Jewish descendant of Abraham is not enough. One must have the moral character of Abraham to be counted among God's chosen and make a conscious decision to follow the Law. "Do not presume to say to yourselves, 'We have Abraham as our father;' for I tell you, God is able from these stones to raise up children to Abraham" (Mt. 3:7; Lk. 3:7).

This severe indictment of the utterly corrupt Jewish society was very characteristic of the Essenes. In the Hymns Scroll, the Jews are regarded as the enemies of the Community. They are called "sea serpents," "dust crawlers" and "serpents that cannot be charmed." Everyone outside the Community was utterly defiled, whereas they with their rigorous strictness were the True Israel.

John the Baptist left Qumran for the Jordan River. While he was there he conducted the greatest spiritual revival of all time. Hundreds of converts flocked to him. The Messianic Age was at hand. The throngs of people returned to the ford day after day hoping to get a glimpse of the Messiah; any day might be the one when the Messiah would appear.

On the day when Jesus appeared, the Baptist was given a sign. The Spirit descended on Jesus and remained on him. John offered to be baptized by Jesus, but Jesus insisted that he be baptized by John and he bowed down before the Baptist. John christened him as the Messiah and, in doing so, represented the blessing of the priests at the Qumran Monastery.

Jesus left John with word he would go into the wilderness to fast for 40 days. Word flew across the world to all the Jews in Diaspora – the Messiah had arrived! The Lord was in the world! Jesus journeyed into the wilderness and to the solitude where he could not be challenged. There he would meditate with the Father.

In the mountains of Jericho, sheltered in one of the natural caves, Jesus fasted for 40 days. Oral tradition says Jesus traveled to the mountains which overlook Jericho, about a two hour walk from the river ford. Many of those who witnessed the christening of the Messiah did not let him out of their sight and followed him into the mountains. Since the Gospels are based on oral tradition, there is no reason to doubt this to be where Jesus traveled. At the end of 40 days Jesus received an unusual visitor. Matthew, Mark and Luke all give accounts of Jesus being visited by the devil. St. John omits this account completely and many other pertinent and important events.

The Synoptic Gospels portray John and his brother James as being among the first disciples to follow Jesus. The Fourth Gospel makes no mention of this. St. John is also portrayed in the Synoptics as among the inner circle of Jesus' disciples, along with Peter and James. Yet the Fourth Gospel gives no account of the transfiguration, an event to which the author was an eyewitness. Even during the Last Supper, John only reluctantly refers to himself in the third person, as "the disciple whom Jesus loved." This is why many reason that the Book of John was written much later after the death of Jesus or by someone other than St. John.

One of the virtues practiced by the Essenes was humility. It was sacrilege to glorify oneself in one's religious writing.

The Teacher of Righteousness is mentioned a mere half-dozen times in all of the scrolls and in none of the writings attributed to him. The Gospels tell that the first to follow Jesus are disciples of John the Baptist. This may offer an explanation for the writing of St. John. The Baptist encouraged James, John, Andrew, Simon, Philip and Nathanael to leave him and follow their new master. All are considered fellow Essenes whom John the Baptist had prepared for the Messiah. St. John, the Essene, was bound by the Law not to honor himself in his own writings.[18]

After 40 days, Jesus received his visitor. This visitor has surely caused as much controversy as any event in the accounts of Christ's ministry. Even considering the supernatural acts which Jesus performed, could it be possible he received a supernatural visitor?

For St. John, Jesus is Messiah from beginning to end. He was in the Father and the Father in him. Surely the Evil One, the Prince of Darkness, would know Jesus was God and it was useless to tempt him.

Luke describes the evil spirit who has dominion over man as "Beelzebub," the "Prince of Demons" and the "power of Darkness." These are in reference to the spirit leader who exercises his dominion over the darkness in the world. The Synoptics all speak of the devil which visited Jesus impersonally as a spirit of acting and not as the spirit leader that exercises his dominion over man. In Lk. 4:1-2: "And Jesus, full of the Holy Spirit returned from the Jordan, and was led by the Spirit for forty days in the wilderness, tempted by *the devil*."

For others such as C.H. Dodd, the temptation of Jesus and his successful completion is the resolution to a personal problem. He wrestles with himself and the challenge as to how he will accept his ministry. He must carry through his newly embraced vocation which is full of menace and of opportunity. He might gain power by exploiting forces of violence to overcome the Roman Empire and liberate his people. He might captivate the multitude with a miracle (the devil suggests throwing himself from the parapet of the Temple).

Dodd suggests that Jesus faced such a challenge and reconciled himself to a course of action prior to beginning his public ministry. Now he could carry out his campaign unhampered by indecision and uncertainty. Dodd suggests that Jesus used this dramatic and symbolic episode to depict this personal and eternal conflict to his disciples.

It is a disservice to Jesus and to Christians to suggest that the Messiah was uncertain which road he was to follow only a few hours before he was to begin his all-important mission — a mission which he was born and raised in the Spirit to perform. Jesus possessed supernatural foreknowledge. He proved this by telling the Samaritan woman at the well everything she had ever done and sending his disciples to catch a fish with a coin in its mouth to pay their Temple tax.

Jesus also demonstrated his foreknowledge in Lk. 22:10-13, when he sent Peter and John to prepare the Last Supper: " 'Behold, when you have entered the city, a man carrying a jar of water will meet you; follow him into the house which he enters, and tell the householder, "The Teacher says to you, Where is the guest room, where I am to eat the passover with my disciples?" And he will show you a large upper room furnished; there make ready.' And they went, and found it as he had told them."

The prophets had foretold of the works of the Messiah. Jesus completely understood and foresaw in its entirety everything that was to happen. Is it possible there could be another explanation?

The priests at Qumran had waited 200 years for the Messiah. This was a very exciting and emotional time for them. John the Baptist, their outside spokesman, had identified and put his blessing along with the official blessing of Qumran on Jesus. Jesus was the Christened One; the Christ, the Messiah. One can imagine the electricity and the feelings of those who were finally going to be rewarded for their faithful deeds. But first, they must visit Jesus and verify that he truly was the Messiah. Then the Messiah must move into the role they had designed for him according to the structured framework of

130

the scrolls.

Jesus' journey into the wilderness was a brilliant maneuver. He spent 40 days in the wilderness. During this time he was isolated from the world and could not be reproached. During these 40 days word had spread over the entire world, that the Messiah had come. The priests could not stop the news from spreading nor could they approach the Messiah until the end of his fasting.

The number 40 held religious significance for the Essenes. It represented a number inspired by God. God caused it to rain for 40 days and 40 nights when He destroyed the earth. God's messenger, Moses, had led the nation of Israel in the wilderness for 40 years. And even in the scrolls, the priests believed the Messiah would be resurrected 40 years following his death to carry out the war against evil. The actions of God were directly related to the number 40.

Jesus' fasting for 40 days had profound meaning for the Essenes. They knew how difficult it was to fast for three days. This man could fast for 40 days! This was one of Jesus' greatest miracles — a feat of superhuman strength only the king-Messiah would be able to perform, a feat meant as a sign for the Essenes and their priesthood.

At the end of 40 days, the Essene priesthood traveled to the mountains outside Jericho. The journey took two hours. John the Baptist was probably in this group. The fact that St. John does not record this event in his Gospel suggests that St. John may also have accompanied the group. However, if St. John did not take part in this visit, it still would have been awkward for him to include an account of this event. He could not very well have referred to the actions of the Essene priesthood as being influenced by the devil when at the same time he was trying to convince them to accept Jesus as the one who fulfilled their ancestors' prophecies.

The priests met Jesus and asked him to perform an act, to give a sign as proof that he was the one for whom they had waited.[19] Jesus had performed one of his greatest miracles but, as so many times later in his ministery, it was not the one which they wanted to see. They ask him to perform a sign according to their expectations. But to do so would have reduced Jesus to a mere instrument to be manipulated by the priesthood. This is exactly what they expected to happen. They reasoned that if he was the true Messiah who was sent by God, he could transform stones into bread. Moses had given their ancestors manna from God in the wilderness. Surely if Jesus was the Messiah he could give them manna just as Moses had done.

Among all the scrolls discovered in the caves at Qumran, by far the most popular reading among the priesthood was the Book of Deuteronomy. More copies of this book were found than any other. When the priests suggested Jesus turn stones to bread he answered them with a scripture from Deuteronomy, one with which they were familiar: "Man does not live by bread alone but that man lives by everything that proceeds out of the mouth of the Lord" (Deut. 8:3).[20]

The priests then took Jesus to Jerusalem and to the southern end of the eastern arcade, at the site of the pinnacle of the Temple. This would seem to be accurately sited at what is currently the southeastern corner of the sanctuary wall. It was from this pinnacle that the Essene priests attempted to throw Jesus, or at least tempted him to throw himself down, with confidence that God would not let him come to harm before his time.

The Law made it a capital crime punishable by death to falsely claim to be the Messiah. The answer was simple for the priests: if they threw Jesus from the pinnacle, God would save him, proving he in fact was the Messiah; if he fell to his death, it was just punishment for a would-be messiah. They challenged him, "If you are the Son of God, throw yourself down; for it is written, 'He will give his angels charge of you' and 'On his hands they will bear you up, lest you strike your foot against a stone'" (Mt. 4:6).[21]

Once again Jesus answered from Deuteronomy, "You shall not put the Lord your God to the test" (Deut. 6:16). There would be other occasions when men would try to take hold of

Jesus to kill him, but they would not succeed. On this particular occasion, he passed his second test.

His final temptation occurred at the Gate of Hope. Here he looked out over the Dead Sea valley, the Jordan River valley, the Mountains of Moab, the Land of Damascus, north to Samaria and west toward Jerusalem and Judea. The priests promised all the countries in the world would be his if he took his place — the place of the Messiah — in their Messianic expectations.

First he would take his place in their Messianic Banquet. The king-Messiah of Israel would take his place as the number two man and pledge his alliance to the Messiah of Aaron. He must bow to the Messiah of Aaron. Symbolically, this meant yielding to the will and the wishes of the Essene priesthood. Only then would the End of Days be ushered in and the King of Israel would take his rightful place over all the lands of the world.

Jesus did not acknowledge the authority of the Essene priests as the authorized interpreters of the Law of Moses. Nor did he acknowledge their interpretation of the End of Days. Jesus interpeted the End of Days to mean the coming of the Kingdom of God on earth, but not as the priesthood had envisioned. Again he quoted Deuteronomy, "You shall fear the Lord your God; you shall serve him and swear by his name" (Deut. 6:13).

The priests knew Jesus was a special being. The way he spoke with authority, his understanding of the Law, the presence which he commanded — all had tremendous influence on the priests. They recognized he was the Messiah. They would have to wait patiently. This was not his time.

Jesus passed all of their tests. He answered their challenges with scriptures which ruled their lives. The prophecies of their ancestors had been fulfilled. The Messiah was in the land. It would be impossible to reverse the news even if they wished to do so. Word had spread over the entire world. As the 40 days drew to a close, crowds gathered to live on his every word.[22] Jesus was ready to begin his ministry.

14

The Ministry of Jesus

"Jesus, when he began his ministery, was 30 years of age" (Lk. 3:23). Reckoning his birth to have occurred in 7 B.C., his years preaching, teaching and healing had begun in A.D. 23. If one accepts the account of Jesus' life as best harmonized around the chronology recorded by John which mentions four successive Passover Feasts, the public ministry of Jesus spanned three full years. Those years culminated in the turbulent events leading to his crucifixion which occurred during the Passover Feast of A.D. 26.

The only scant information recorded about the first year of Jesus' ministry is supplied by the Gospel John. Immediately after his ordeal in the Judean wilderness, Jesus returned where John the Baptist was ministering at the River Jordan. There he found his first disciples whom John had prepared for the Messiah and whom he readily released to follow Jesus.

Here at the Jordan, Jesus celebrated his first year's ministry as a baptizing ministry beside John the Baptist. During this first year, St. John records Jesus' initial visit to Jerusalem for the Passover. Jesus displayed his tremendous human strength and determination by invading the Temple area, where the priests controlled the traffic of money changers and sellers of sacrificial animals. He drove them out of his Father's house.

Jesus saw the Temple priesthood as corrupt. He believed they had desecrated the Temple with their sacrilegious practices.

While in Jerusalem, Jesus performed many miracles and attracted considerable attention. One miraculous fete impressed a man named Nicodemus who came to Jesus in the secrecy of the night. Jesus challenged Nicodemus to become a follower, "Ye must be born again." One is not born into the Kingdom of God simply by being born a Jew; one must make a conscious decision to live the life of a moral Jew according to the Law of God. Those who follow Jesus' teaching must be born of the Spirit.

During the subsequent baptizing ministry in the Jordan, Jesus attracted so many people that John's disciples became envious. To help ease the discontent, Jesus and his disciples left for Galilee via Samaria. It was here he encountered the Samaritan woman at the well near Sychar. The journey to Galilee was delayed while Jesus held his first unscheduled revival. At the close of his first year of ministry, Jesus still remained largely unknown.

Popularity marked the second year of Jesus' ministry. When he arrived in Galilee he visited his home and the synagogue. He then boldly announced that he had come to fulfill the Messianic prophecy of Isa. 61. Vast throngs in Galilee gathered in response to his ministry. Many were healed. The complement of 12 disciples representing the leaders of the 12 tribes of Israel, were chosen. All were Galileans except one, Judas Iscariot, who was a Judean,[1] and Jesus bestowed them all with apostolic authority.

His fame and popularity continued to grow during this second year. As many as 5,000 people gathered on a single occasion to hear him teach. During this lengthy phase of his ministry Jesus traveled to Jerusalem, as did every faithful Jew, to observe the Passover in Jerusalem. During this visit, Jesus healed a lame man on the Sabbath, but this act created such hostility that the Jews sought to kill him. So he returned to Galilee where his fame was abounding to heal the multitudes and teach them the way to enter the Kingdom of Heaven.

The third year became the turning point in Jesus' ministry. His fame accelerated to a climax capped with his miracle multiplication of the loaves and fishes to feed the throng. At this point Jesus began to speak in plain terms to the crowd. He would not be the militant leader who would overthrow the Roman rulers. Instead, entry into his kingdom would be costly. He himself must be put to death. The crowds began to melt away. He asked his disciples if they also intended to leave him. Jesus continued to minister in Galilee but the mood of the crowds had changed. Finally, he left his home and his great year of spectacular popularity.

Much of the last six months of his final year was spent across the Jordan in Perea. In this area Jesus drew new crowds who gathered to receive his message and his blessings. He met the cheering, exuberant throngs with requirements of total commitment and spelled out the demands of discipleship.

Jesus crossed the Jordan at the time of the Passover and traveled once again into Jerusalem, to fulfill the prophecies. Palm Sunday was the open declaration to the world that Jesus was entering Jerusalem as the Messiah. This week was filled with encounters with scribes and Pharisees. Here he prophesied the destruction of the Temple and his own resurrection. A plot against him by the Sanhedrin resulted in his arrest, conviction and crucifixion at the hands of the Roman soldiers.

Jesus belonged to an era when his followers believed in the End of Days. Their thinking was quite different than that of today's. The meaning of "messiah" is difficult to comprehend in today's world. Jesus was not just a teacher who crowned his life's work with martyrdom. Jesus was from his birth until his crucifixion, the Messiah. He was imbued with the messianic expectation of his age and he regarded himself as the one chosen to fulfill it.

Jesus could be humorous. He could be whimsical. He had great wisdom. He was brilliant in debate and capable of answering the most difficult questions and silencing his opponents. When someone would try to trick him in an argument — an event that often happened at first — Jesus adopted a humble attitude and deftly led the challenger on until he was caught in his own trap. Jesus enjoyed this — and at the same time he was compassionate. He was not always tranquil; often his wrath erupted on the Pharisees.

During his ministry, his portrait as a teacher is the one most vividly portrayed in the Gospels. Matthew's Gospel says he taught as one having his own authority. In his own words, "I come not to destroy but to fulfill" the Torah. But even the necessity of this statement demonstrates the distance he had traveled.

His disciples most often referred to him as "Teacher." This is true as well in the Gospel of Mark which includes very few of his formal teachings. He was addressed as "Rabbi" by his immediate followers and by strangers who included those who themselves claimed the same title. His method of teaching was most engaging. His points were driven home with fables or parables — illustrations which were immediately understood.

The Essene priesthood was ascetic but Jesus was not. He was friendly to publicans and sinners. He freely accepted hospitality. When asked to account for these actions, he whimsically pointed out that those who are whole need no physician. He spent his time with the sick.

The Sermon on the Mount occurred shortly after Jesus' formal ministry began. He had already been baptized by John. He had timed his return from his period of fasting in the Judean wilderness to correspond with the Passover of the Jews. Word of the coming of the Messiah had spread throughout the entire world. Thousands had journeyed to Qumran to celebrate the annual Feast of the Passover. When Jesus returned, the Essene community was waiting to receive his every word. "And when he saw the crowds, he went up on the mountain, and when he sat down his disciples came to him" (Mt. 5:11).

The Sermon is presented intact by St. Matthew. St. Luke also records these same teachings with almost identical wording scattered throughout his Gospel. Many scholars believe the sayings of Jesus in Matthew and Luke are derived from

"Q." The Essene scribes were capable of recording his teachings in the exact words and spirit in which he spoke them. The reference which both Luke and Matthew used can be trusted as accurate. Although these scrolls have never been identified, they contain the exact words of Jesus.

St. John wrote his Gospel as a message to the Essene community. He did not include any of the sayings of Jesus nor did he include instructions on discipleship. There was no need to familiarize the Essenes with the thoughts of Jesus. John's purpose is to persuade the Community that the Light is come into the world and the Kingdom of God is here.

The Sermon on the Mount was Jesus' introduction to the Essene community. He presented himself and what he stood for in this first example of his unusually successful teaching. As Jesus began his ministry, those who followed him regarded him as upholding the Law of Moses. "Think not that I am come to destroy the Law, or the prophets; I am not come to destroy, but to fulfill...not an iota, not a dot, will pass from the law until all is accomplished" (Mt. 5:17-18).

The length of the Sermon, as it is recorded in Matthew, indicates its importance. This, the most familiar collection of Jesus' teachings, includes the Beatitudes, the Lord's Prayer, his instructions to love one's enemy, and the Golden Rule. Many have found the Sermon on the Mount to be the most ethical statement of all time. Others dismiss its intent as unrealistic. Still others believe Jesus meant this as a heroic lifestyle only to be aspired to by his disciples until the End of Days.

The key to the religious and historical understanding of the Sermon on the Mount is given in Mt. 5:43: "You have heard that it has been said, 'You shall love your neighbors, and hate your enemy.' But I say unto you 'Love your enemies.'"

If you love only those who love you,
　　what credit is that to you?
　　　　Even sinners love those who love them.

If you do good only to those who do good to you,
  what credit is that to you?
    Even sinners do as much.

And if you lend only where you expect to be repaid
  what credit is that to you?
    Even sinners lend to sinners, to be repaid in full.

But you must love your enemies and do good,
  and lend without expecting any return;
And you will have a rich reward:
  You will be sons of the Most High
    because He is kind to the ungrateful and the wicked.

Those who heard these words had already been taught to hate their enemies. Nowhere in Jewish tradition or in the Old Testament is there any command to hate one's enemies. The concept is found in the Qumran writings. There it is written in QS I:3-4, "To love everyone whom God has elected, and hate everyone whom he has rejected...to hate all the sons of darkness, each according to his sinfulness in the revenge of God."[2]

The priests at Qumran consistently demonstrated their policy to tighten the Mosaic Law. They believed that the near eschatology and the final consumption were at hand, and hence the formation of the Community and its regulations for purity under the Law which approached a monastic ideal. Jesus aimed at his auditors' eschatology. He wanted to soften it. His command transformed their law for hatred for the enemy into one of brotherly love. The Mosaic Law had been made more stringent to hasten the coming of the End of Days. Jesus brought relief to his followers: "For my yoke is easy, and my burden is light" (Mt. 11:30).

The Law was not abolished by the words of Jesus, but his interpretations of the Law presented to his followers in the

140

Sermon on the Mount supported the ethical core of the Law and not a sharpening of externalities. He eliminated the emphasis on incidental provisions of the Law to show that the eschatological event was not dependent on the human will; man is not the instrument of revenge.

The Beatitudes indicate Jesus' conscious effort to state a positive attitude toward the Essene community. To the Poor in Spirit he promised nothing less than the Kingdom of Heaven, — participation in the Kingdom of God. "Poor," as found in Mt. 5:3 and in Lk. 6:20, in no way presumes the destitute are called blessed. The Hebrew equivalent to "in spirit" is the word "ruah," which not only means "spirit," but also "agreement" or "choice." The usual translation of "Poor in Spirit" is incorrect. It means "poor by choice," "poor in inward agreement" or "voluntarily poor." This then is the true sense of this passage.

Jesus counted those as "blessed" whose worldly goods mean nothing. In so doing, Jesus reinforced one of the major tenants of the Essene movement. Both the Manual of Discipline and Josephus testify to this Essene tenant. The members of the Community call themselves "ebionim," which means the "poor ones." In the Hymns Scroll as well, a single member is referred to as "ebyon," or "a poor one." Their contempt for money was one of their chief principles. The Essenes accepted "the Poor" as a proper name for their church. Based on the introduction of the Sermon on the Mount alone, it would seem highly improbable that the audience consisted of anyone unfamiliar with Essene teaching.

Jesus draws several parallels when referring to Essene teachings. With regard to the disciples as the "light of the world" (Mt. 5:14-16), a direct reference is made to one that can be found in the Manual of Discipline as well as in other writings: "All the sons of justice tread in the ways of light" (QS III:20).

In Mt. 5:20, Jesus demands that the righteous must exceed the scribes and the Pharisees, or else they will not enter the Kingdom of Heaven. In QS V:19 it says that one must be more scrupulous with the Law than the Pharisees. Open opposition to the Pharisees, particularly their interpretation of the Law, is recorded in QS V:41.

In Mt. 5:20 and again in Mt. 5:33 Jesus begins, "You have heard that it was said to the men of old..." This description of past generations as "of old" or "of the beginning" has its parallel in the Damascus Document. "The earlier ones who have gone into the covenant...and God was mindful of his covenant with the earlier ones" (CD IV:10, VIII:4).

Reference can be made to the Community life of the Essenes as a parallel to the words spoken by Jesus about he who is angry with his brother in Mt. 5:22. "Brother" in this passage refers to a brother in the religious family, not to a natural brother. The Manual of Discipline often witnesses to this kind of love which one must have for his brother.

In Mt. 5:28 the provision in the Law against adultery is sharpened to include the Essene ideal of self-denial: "But I say unto you, that whosoever looketh upon a woman to lust after her hath committed adultery with her already in his heart." In QS I:6 one finds, "...stubbornness of a sinful heart and eyes of unchastity;" again in QHAB V:7, "...those who do not lust after their eyes;" and in CD III:3, "...thoughts of sinful lusts and eyes of wantonness."

The Qumran priesthood also enforced their ruling for the indissolubility of marriage. One reads in CD VII:2, "Whoredom by taking two wives during their lifetime..." Addressing the issue of divorce, this passage is in direct contradiction to rabbinic law which permitted divorce. Jesus' confrontation with the Pharisees in Mt. 19:3-9 directly parallels the teachings of the Essenes. Jesus cites Genesis 1:27, as does the author of the Damascus Document: "The basic principle of creation is 'Male and female created He them.'"

Jesus professes a radical rejection of oaths in Mt. 5:33-37. This also has its parallel in Essenism. Josephus writes of the Essenes' refusal to swear an oath: "Their word once given means more to them than an oath. They refrain from swearing, for they hold it worse than perjury. They say that no man

142

who is not believed unless he call upon the divinity is already condemned in advance." CD XIX:1 declares: "It is forbidden to swear by God's name."

Jesus issued an extraordinary statement in Mt. 5:38. Here he commands his followers to turn the other cheek, rather than resist evil. A parallel in QS X:17 states: "I will not repay a man with evil, I will follow the man of power with good, for God has judgment over all life, and he repays each according to his works." The Essenes attitude of hatred toward their enemies which was discussed earlier had an eschatological character. It is also evident that their reason for not striking back in their case of personal forgiveness of "men of power" is because they relied on God's punishment.

Jesus rejected eschatological hatred and also went further in his condemnation of hatred toward personal enemies. He insisted his followers reject the principle of measure for measure; to forget revenge entirely. Jesus commanded, "You, therefore, must be perfect." It's no wonder that many consider the demands of Jesus and his intentions as unrealistic. Matthew, however, does not consider them unrealistic. Matthew's use of "perfect" does not represent the absence of imperfection. Rather, it means complete devotion, single-mindedness. This is the kind of perfection that must be applied to discipleship. "If you would be perfect, go, sell what you possess and give to the poor, and you will have treasure in heaven; and come, follow me" (Mt. 19:21).

Do not worry about material things.
    Anxiety of this sort, beside being useless and unnecessary,
        spoils the joy you ought to take in living.

Observe different forms of nature – the birds and flowers:
    They do not worry about the cost of finery;
        Yet even the regal Solomon was not better arrayed.

Understand what is really vital:
The Kingdom of God and how to serve it;
Everything else will take its proper place
and you will not be disturbed by a bad sense of proportion.

Do not make long prayers, asking God for foolish things.
He knows what is good for you better than you do
and needs no prompting to keep Him interested.

When you pray,
try to understand what it is God wants from you;
It is much more important
than what you want from God.

Jesus taught them to pray. His prayer is tense and eschatological: "May the end of the world come now and Thy will be done! Give us each day what we need to sustain us until the morrow. When the end comes, may we not be led into temptation or trial, or have to undergo the probation of suffering."

He taught that religion can be summed up in two principles: "Love God sincerely and other people as much as you love yourself." The entire sermon is summarized in Mt. 7:12: "So whatever you wish that men would do to you, do so to them." He did not invent these summaries of the "Law and the Prophets," but by selecting them, he makes his emphasis clear.

"And when Jesus finished these sayings, the crowds were astonished at his teaching, for he taught them as one who had authority, and not as their scribes" (Mt. 7:28).

Jesus shows he is versed in Essene thought in the Sermon on the Mount. He also assumes his opponents among the

Pharisees are familiar with Essene thought as well. In Mt. 12:9-14, Mk. 3:1-6 and Lk. 6:6-11 Jesus reproaches the Pharisees after healing the man with the withered hand on the Sabbath. He tells them that they have no right to criticize the healing as they all would not hesitate to rescue a sheep which had fallen into the pit on the Sabbath. The Damascus Document specifically forbids such action: "If the animal falls into a pit, it may not be drawn out on the Sabbath."

Rules for the Sabbath were markedly more strict than those of the Pharisees. However, in a life threatening situation a man's life could be saved on the Sabbath: "But should any man fall into water or fire, let him be pulled out with the aid of a ladder or rope or some such tool." To cure a man on the Sabbath was forbidden by the Pharisees, but it was much more strictly forbidden by the Qumran priesthood.

The Pharisees saw in Jesus the Essene Messiah[3] even though he did not claim the title. On one occasion, the Pharisees brought a woman to him who had been caught in the act of adultery. "They said to him: 'Now Moses in the Law commanded us, that such should be stoned: but what sayest though?' This they said tempting him, that they might have to accuse him" (Jn. 8:5-6).

They hoped Jesus would take the responsibility of pronouncing a ferocious interpretation of the Law of Moses, (one not enforced at that time), or be forced to take a stand against the Law of Moses. Characteristically, Jesus shifted the decision back onto the crowd. He corroborated the stoning with the condition: "That one of you who is faultless must throw the first stone." After the crowd had left, Jesus spoke: "No more do I condemn you. Go and sin no more."

Jesus made it clear from the beginning of his ministry he would not follow Essene thought in all situations. He rejected all excessive features of the Law, such as eschatological hatred or the anxious pedantry of the priests. Whenever their meaning of a rule had been perverted into its opposite by the Essene's eschatological yearning, such as their tightening of the Sabbath regulations, Jesus provided his sharpest rejections with teachings and actions diametrically opposed. Often he criticized the Qumran priesthood and their interpretation of the Law by chastising the Pharisees for the same account, even though their practice may not have been as severe as that of the Essene priests.[4]

When Jesus began his baptizing ministry, it was considered more successful than that of John's. John was already baptizing in Aenon, not far from Salim, because of the abundance of water. His disciples became concerned because more people were going to Jesus. The Gospels report that Jesus and his followers left the Jordan River because of possible friction with John's disciples. "Now when the Lord knew that the Pharisees had heard that Jesus was making and baptizing more disciples than John, he left Judea and departed to Galilee" (Jn. 4:1-3).

It may have been the increased interest on the part of the Pharisees that caused Jesus to depart, but acording to Mark, a more probable cause was the arrest of John by Herod Antipas. During the winter months, Antipas lived in his castle at Machaerus, which was near the Dead Sea, on the east side of the Jordan River valley, overlooking the very bank where John and Jesus baptized their converts. From there, he could view from his fortress the throngs that made their way to the river. It wasn't difficult for him to discover that the men responsible for the crowds were also to be the key participants in a movement that would come into power and rule the world.

Matthew says that Herod had John arrested because the Baptist had criticized Herod for his marrying his brother's wife, Herodias. Josephus reports another reason: "Herod was terrified of John's influence with the people. He feared it might lead to an uprising, for they all seemed ready to do anything at his instigation. So he thought it much better to forestall any subversive action he might take, and get rid of him."[5]

There may be yet another reason. Herod was not a religious man, a better description would be superstitious. And although he did not follow the Law, he had respect for the

146

prophets. Herod knew the stories of the new kingdom that was to come. He considered John to be a great prophet and one of the keys to this reputed new kingdom. If he could control the keys to the movement, Herod would have to be dealt with, giving him leverage in the new order.

Herod feared John, for he knew John was a righteous and holy man, and kept him safe. When John talked to him he was perplexed; yet he heard him gladly. John was even allowed visitations by his disciples. For John, the actions of Jesus were not conforming to his expectations. He was bewildered at the manner in which Jesus was fulfilling his mission. John himself was to play a major role in the End of Days. When John learned of the deeds of Christ from his disciples, he became anxious to see Jesus appear as the Messiah. Impatiently, he sent a message to Jesus to help prompt him.

The greatest challenge to Jesus' ministry came in the form of this message from John carried by his disciples: "Are you he who is to come, or shall we look for another?" (Mt. 11:3). Jesus, who was given the blessing of the Essene community and recognized as the Chosen One through John's baptism, now was being challenged as to his motives. This challenge by John must also have appeared to the crowd as representing the position of the Essene priesthood.

Jesus answered by quoting from Isa. 35:5-6, a verse well familiar to John, "Go and tell John what you hear and see: the blind receive their sight and the lame walk, lepers are cleansed and the deaf hear, and the dead are raised up, and the poor have the good news preached to them" (Mt. 11:4-6). But Jesus changed the end of the verse in his message to John and the priesthood. He emphasized particularly the preaching of good news to "the Poor," the Essene church. Instead of the Messiah coming in glory, with displays of tremendous power, Jesus substituted a spiritual reign of charity. The Messianic kingdom will not be the one John had envisioned.

After John's disciples had left, Jesus asked the crowds concerning John: "What did you go out into the wilderness to behold? A reed shaken by the wind? Why then did you go out?

147

To see a man clothed in soft raiment? Behold, those who wear soft raiment are in king's houses. Why then did you go out? To see a prophet? Yes, I tell you, and more than a prophet. This is he of whom it is written 'Behold I send my messenger before thy face, who shall prepare the way before thee' " (Mt. 11:7-10).

But the crowds were not there to see John. They had come to see Jesus. He asked them why they had come and what had they expected to see. Was he not performing as the Messiah, according to the scriptures? He even confirmed John as the messenger in Isaiah who shall prepare the way for the Messiah. Jesus had answered John's question.

Herod was tricked into beheading John. John's disciples then went to Herod and requested their leader's body: "And his disciples came and took the body and buried it; and they went and told Jesus" (Mt. 14:12, Mk. 6:29).

The cemetery at Qumran has never been fully excavated. If it was to be excavated, archeologists would find that the Essenes buried their dead according to rank. Each man's standing played a role in everything he did. If the hierarchy of the cemetery could be established, there, near the highest ranking, lays a skeleton either without a skull or one with the skull severed at the neck. John's disciples buried him along with his fellow brothers to be raised again in the final days.

Herod then tried to secure the other key to the kingdom. But Jesus was warned: "Get away from here, Herod wants to kill you" (Lk. 13:31).[6] Jesus heeded this warning and left Herod's country and journeyed to Galilee.

After this short trip to Galilee, Jesus went up to Jerusalem for the Passover of the Jews. "In the temple he found those who were selling oxen and sheep and pigeons, and the moneychangers at their business. And making a whip of cords, he drove them all, with the sheep and oxen, out of the temple" (Jn. 2:14,15).[7]

The Temple Mount[8] was the scene of the clash between Jesus and the ecclesiastical rulers who controlled sacrificial and other rituals of the Temple.[9] The point of this commerce was the lower area of the Hanuyot, the lower area of the Temple Mount where thousands of sacrificial lambs were penned and traded for the benefit of the pilgrims. The most prestigious function of the Hanuyot was to serve as the seat for the Sanhedrin.[10] It also allowed money changers and other dealers of ritual objects to operate on the lower levels. Many puritanical pilgrims regarded the Hanuyot as a sacred area.[11]

What archeologists have been able to discover in the Hanuyot has given New Testament historians a vast appreciation for John's testimony. The Synoptic accounts give similar references to the money changers and venders of doves. Only in John does the story take on a different character. He describes the presence of sheep and oxen, and the making of a whip. John's account has helped to explain the varied functions and divisions of the Hanuyot by describing the magnitude of the cleansing of the Temple.[12]

In the Synoptic Gospels, the cleansing of the Temple occurred at the end of Jesus' ministry on his last journey to Jerusalem, just before his death. In their narrative, the entire ministry is condensed into one year or less and the cleansing can logically only be placed near the end of his ministry.

In John, the cleansing took place during the first year of Jesus' ministry. It is more logical for Jesus to have projected early on an image of anti-establishment; an image that was strongly anti-Temple. John has deepened the opposition to the Temple Mount — a viewpoint that is perfectly plausible in light of the Essene sentiments toward the Hellenistic movement, a group within Jewry that was compromising and welding the Jewish religion to Roman paganism.[13]

After the cleansing of the Temple, Jesus faced a similar challenge as the one presented by John the Baptist. In the synagogue in Capernaum, he met a man who had the spirit of an unclean demon. The demon asked, "Ah! What have you to do with us, Jesus of Nazareth? Have you come to destory us? I know who you are, 'the Holy One of God' " (Lk. 4:34).

This challenged Jesus to take a stand; he would have to admit that he was the Messiah. But Jesus did not want to publicly claim to be the Messiah; to do so would bind him to the expectations and writings of the Essene priesthood. If he claimed to be the Messiah and did not perform according to these expectations, he would then be branded as not living in the Spirit of truth. Jesus left the decision to each member of the Community as to whether he was fulfilling the prophecies. They had witnessed his deeds and heard his words, and they knew the writings of the prophets.

A claim by Jesus to be the Messiah would also sentence him to the danger of death. The Pharisees had welded the Jewish religion to that of the Romans. Because their continued power depended on their support of the Roman Empire, they became concerned about a leader rising among the common people and stirring political unrest. The high priest, Caiaphas, believed it expedient that one man should die for the people so that the whole nation should not perish. "He prophesied that Jesus should die for that nation" (Jn. 11:51).

During the third year of his ministry, Jesus was confronted in Jerusalem by the Jews: "If you be the Christ, tell us plainly" (Jn. 10:24). Jesus answered, saying: "I told you, and ye believed not: the works I do in my Father's name, they bear witness to me" (Jn. 10:25).

These words meant blasphemy to the Jews. They tried to stone him but he escaped. He performed the signs but they refused to see. He answered their questions but they failed to listen. Jesus continued to be challenged about his identity throughout the rest of his ministry.

The third year marked the turning point of Jesus' ministry. During the previous years, his fame had accelerated and his popularity continued to grow. Thousands followed Jesus because they saw the miracles he performed.

At the time of the Passover, Jesus went up into a mountain and sat with his disciples. There were so many people — an estimated 5,000 — that the disciples did not have enough money to buy food for everyone. The disciples found a young lad with five barley loaves and two small fishes and presented these to Jesus. "And Jesus took the loaves; and when he had given thanks, he distributed to the disciples, and the disciples to them that were set down; and likewise of the fishes as much as they would eat" (Jn. 6:11).

The Passover is also called the "feast of unleavened bread." As it was then celebrated, the festival referred to manna from heaven that God had once sent down and would do so again. When Jesus finished the miraculous feeding he fled the crowd because "they were about to come and take him by force, to make him a king" (Jn. 6:15). They had witnessed this sign and they agreed he must be the prophet who would come into the world to lead them as the king-Messiah of Israel.

When Jesus encountered the same crowd the following day, he chastened them for their lack of insight. Instead of seeking more free food, he told them that they should be seeking food of another kind: "Do not labor for the food which perisheth, but for that food which endureth unto everlasting life, which the Son of man shall give unto you: for him hath God the Father sealed" (Jn. 6:27).

The crowd asked what they could do to perform the work of God and receive eternal life. Jesus responded that the work of God is to have faith in the one whom God has sent. Then the crowd demanded another sign from Jesus to prove that he was indeed the one sent by God. As had happened so many times before in his ministry, he was asked to verify his identity. On the previous day this same crowd had witnessed a miracle with the multiplication of the loaves but had failed to comprehend its meaning. Now they requested further proof. They quoted a passage from scripture: "What work do you perform? Our fathers were given manna in the desert; as it is written, 'He gave them bread from heaven to eat' " (Jn. 6:30-31).

But Jesus replied: "My Father gives the true bread from heaven. For the bread of God is that which comes down from heaven, and gives life to the world" (Jn. 6:32-33). Jesus meant that he was the true bread that was sent down from heaven by the Father; but the crowd interpreted his words literally — a promise that God would send them all the life-giving bread

151

they would ever need. Although Jesus spoke metaphorically, the crowd took his words literally. Believing that Jesus had agreed to provide this endless supply of bread, they asked, "Lord, give us this bread always" (Jn. 6:34). Jesus acknowledged, "I am the bread of life: he that comes to me shall never hunger; and he that believeth on me shall never thirst" (Jn. 6:35).

As his words became more revealing, the crowd moved farther from understanding. "I am the bread of life. Your ancestors ate the manna in the desert, but died. But the bread which comes down from heaven is such that whoever eats it will not die. I am the living bread which came down from heaven. If anyone eats this bread he will live forever. The bread which I will give him is my flesh, which I give so that the world may live" (Jn. 6:48-51).

The crowd became thoroughly sickened. How could he offer his flesh for them to eat? They that only the day before were ready to make Jesus their king, were now thoroughly scandalized. Many of his followers said: "This teaching is too hard. Who can listen to this?" (Jn. 6:60). They turned away and did not follow him again.

The Gospel of John tells how, through misunderstanding, the distance continues to widen between Jesus and his followers due to his increasing use of irony and double meanings. John's discourses develop themes that interpret Jesus' signs, but only for his readers. John portrays those who oppose Jesus as people who live in the darkness. In John's writing, Jesus does not teach the crowd; his Gospel is intended for the reader-believer. The crowd's misunderstanding acts as a foil to heighten the belief of the reader.[14]

Jesus asked his disciples if they, too, would leave him: "Does this make you want to give up? What gives life is the Spirit; the flesh is of no use at all. The words I have spoken to you are Spirit and life" (Jn. 61-63). Peter answered: "You have the words that give eternal life. And now we believe and know that you are the Holy One from God" (Jn. 6:68-69).

Jesus left his homeland, Galilee, for the last time. And

after ministering in Perea for six months, he and his disciples made their last journey together to Jerusalem. Five days before the Passover, Jesus made his way into Jerusalem. The crowds greeted him to the shout of "Hosanna! Blessed is He who comes in the name of the Lord, the King of Israel" (Jn. 12:13). Jesus had promised his followers he would return "in clouds with great power and glory," and gather "the elect" who have remained faithful all these years from the ends of the earth (Mk. 13:24-27).

For his greeters, Jesus is initiating the final confrontation that will usher in this new kingdom. He has come to Jerusalem as the king-Messiah of Israel to claim his throne and to display his kingly power. What they have patiently waited for is about to come to pass.

Before the Passover Feast, the time had come for Jesus to prepare a final meal for his followers. During the meal, Jesus gave a sign to one of the disciples, Judas Iscariot. Jesus had sent him away expeditiously and told him: "Do quickly what you are going to do" (Jn. 13:27). The devil entered Judas as he left the room. None of the other disciples understood his actions. We are told that, "Some had an idea, since Judas had charge of the money-bag, that Jesus said to him, 'Buy what we need for the Passover Feast' or 'Give something to the poor.' Then at once, after taking the bit of bread, he went out. It was then night" (Jn. 13:29-30).

This devil which entered Judas was the devil of self-prestige — the passion of self-glorification. On many occasions Jesus counseled his disciples individually. On one such occasion, he had arranged a preconceived sign that would designate the disciple whom he had chosen to help usher in his kingdom. The one he had counseled on this account was Judas. During the meal, the others knew nothing of this sign. Even Judas was not aware that the others were unknowing of the purpose of this act. Not until Jesus designated him did he know that he was the one who would help to bring about the Messianic kingdom.

Judas, as the others, had no understanding of the true

kingdom that Jesus would bring to the earth. The devil that entered into him was the opportunity for him to rise above the others as the champion of the Messiah. Humilty was one of the virtues manifested in the Essene doctrine for those who live in the ways of the light. It was believed that no one must do anything to set himself above any of the others. But for Judas, this was his chance to record his name in history as one of the greatest Jews of all time.

In analyzing the Gospels, one of the more significant events that occurred at the start of this century was a movement to remove Jesus from the literary context of the Gospel writers and view him instead from a historical perspective. Scholars such as Renan made considerable progress, but the scholar who produced this hiatus more than any other was Albert Schweitzer. In his book entitled *The Quest of the Historic Jesus*, first published in 1906, he advanced a thesis that Jesus considered himself the Messiah and brought death upon himself in the expectation it would bring on a "parousia" — a Greek word meaning "to become present, arrive, the hour in which the Messiah would be seen as such" — a manifestation that he himself was the king-Messiah of Israel.[15] This idea that the Messiah must be "the suffering servant of God" was prophesied by Isaiah. On the basis of Jesus' own disclosures, he sought death to bring about his Messiahship and the Kingdom of God.

The selection of Judas Iscariot as one of the disciples had an intentional purpose from the very beginning.[16] All 12 were Galileans except Judas, who was a Judean. "While I was with them I kept them safe by the power of your name, the name you gave me. I protected them, and not one of them was lost, except the man who was bound to be lost — that the scripture might come true" (Jn. 17:12). Jesus knew from the onset the role which Judas was to play. Judas saw himself acting out an essential part to Jesus' plans. He did not inform the authorities for money. The "thirty pieces of silver" meant nothing to him. He was destined to be the leader of the tribe of Judah. It was necessary that he accept a sum only to seal the contract

154

with the Sanhedrin.

The tense and complex situation in Jerusalem on the eve of the Passover speaks volumes. Moreover, it is difficult to understand why Jesus was arrested and charged with a capital crime punishable by death. The historic data provides an entirely different, and more realistic, background to the history of Jesus' trial and execution.

What were the grounds for this concern by the Sanhedrin and what were the charges brought against Jesus on which the council condemned him to death? Some believe the charges resulted from Jesus' raising Lazarus from death. Others believe he represented a threat to the establishment after he cleansed the Temple.

When Jesus crossed the Jordan and entered Judea for this final confrontation with the religious leaders of Jerusalem, he stayed at Bethany just outside of the city. Here he performed one last, crowning miracle. Lazarus, already in the tomb four days, was raised from the dead (Jn. 11:17-44). Jesus had conquered disease, demons, storms, and now even death. This last miracle may have brought the fanatical hatred of the Jewish leaders to a boiling point. The wonder of Jesus threatened their grip on the people (Jn. 11:45-54).

Others believe it was the cleansing of the Temple that caused the grounds for the charges against Jesus. Jesus' trial did not result from a quarrel with money changers. Nor does one pay with his life for such an incident. They see the cleansing as an attack on the high priests and aristocracy of Jerusalem and view it as a threat to the very power center. They believe this caused the drastic action by the Sanhedrin. However, in all probability (and according to John) the cleansing took place during the first year of Jesus' ministry and did not occur shortly before his death.

Still others theorize that Jesus may have been a Galilean revolutionary and Zealot and charged, prosecuted, and sentenced as one. His life had followed and preceded revolutionary trends in Israel. The Zealot's revolutionary movement was not only directed against the Romans but often against their established religious authorities and their social evils. The Zealots clung to their own ethical standards and social ideals. They had adherents among the Essenes because they also dreamed of a final war that would redeem them.

It may have been any one or a combination of these events which caused the authorities to become concerned. Yet there is one other event that caused the Sanhedrin's concern and this constituted the grounds for their actions. Jesus had celebrated his Messianic Banquet!

Jesus' last meal was not a Passover meal. Due to the development of the Synoptic tradition, the night of Jesus' arrest has become a mere historization of the true story. The Gospel passages must be subjected to historical criticism to determine the facts related to this last meal and its true nature.

The description of Jesus' last meal in the Gospels contains no reference to a Passover setting. The Feast of the Passover meal is a family meal. Jesus shares his last meal only with his 12 disciples — his closed and narrow group. This behavior is not characteristic of Jesus, nor would a Passover meal call for such a restricted arrangement. It is customary at the Passover meal for the "pater familias" to give the opening blessing and someone else, a guest of honor, to offer the closing benediction over the "cup of blessing." Yet, according to our accounts, Jesus delivers both benedictions. In Mark, the two blessings are side by side at the beginning of the meal, which does not corroborate the Passover meal.

It is exactly these features, peculiar to Jesus' last meal and unexplainable by Passover customs, that find their parallels in the Essene cult meal described in the texts of Qumran. Here it is given that only those of the inner circle, the full members of the Order, participate in the meal. Presiding over the Essene meal is not a "pater familias," but a properly anointed leader of the Community. The Essene leader pronounces both blessings over bread and wine, and both are given together at the beginning of the meal. Thus, there is no specific indication of a Passover setting.

The Gospel accounts of Jesus' last meal have several features which are unexplainable as a Passover meal but directly correspond to the Essene cult meal. The Essene cult meal was celebrated in anticipation of a final banquet "when God brings the Messiah with them." Josephus writes of the Essene cult meal:

"After the purification, they assemble in a special room which none of the uninitiated is permitted to enter; pure now themselves, they repair to the refectory, as to some sacred shrine. When they have seated themselves in silence, the baker serves the loaves in order, and the cook sets before each one place with a single course. Before the meal, the priest gives the blessing and it is unlawful to partake before the prayer."

According to Josephus, silence during the Essene meals is based on the regulation that they may only speak in due order: "They speak in turn, each making way for the other." In QS VI:10, "No man shall interrupt the speech of the other before his brother has finished speaking. Nor shall he speak out of his rank." And in QS VI:4, "Each is to sit before him according to his rank."

In Lk. 22:24, "A dispute also arose among them, which of them was to be regarded as the greatest." John's Gospel, throws a light on the last meal with Jesus. Here it describes John, "the Beloved Disciple," as always standing in rank above Peter. In Jn. 13:24, Peter could not ask the Lord who the traitor was — he was not permitted to speak out of turn. Peter gave a signal to John, who held a more honored place than Peter, that "the Beloved Disciple" should ask the question. This behavior is understandable in view of this provision in the Essene writings. John, who was the youngest among the disciples and about the same age as Jesus, must have also had the most formal training to be regarded as holding the highest rank among the disciples.

According to John, the Last Supper did not take place on the Jewish Passover. In the Synoptics, Jesus was arrested on the eve of his crucifixion, and the events leading to his death

157

occurred in rapid succession. In Mark 15:25, "And it was the third hour and they crucified him." According to the division of time, the "third hour" in the Ancient East was 9 a.m., and "...at the ninth hour" (3 p.m.) the tragedy came to an end. So, between the early morning hours when Jesus was arrested and 9 a.m., he was transferred to the Sanhedrin, his trial and condemnation were carried out and he was taken to Pontius Pilate who sent him to Herod. After a period of time Jesus was returned to Pilate and then sentenced, condemned, and marched to Calvary where he was crucified. All of this could not have been accomplished during only a few hours of a single night.

The Sanhedrin was regulated by the Mishnah which held that in capital cases the trial be held during the daytime.[17] This rule of long standing was in force at that time. The Mishnah also stated that trials may not be held on the eve of the Sabbath or the eve of a festival. Also, a verdict could not be delivered until the day after the trial.[18] All of this suggests that Jesus was not arrested on the eve of his death. The meal he shared with his disciples was not the Passover meal. His comment, "from now on I shall not drink from the vine until the kingdom comes," suggests that the time that expired was more than a few hours.

Members of the Order of the Essene priesthood went into their refectory "as to some sacred shrine." This special room, the dining hall for their cult meals, has been uncovered by excavation at Khirbet Qumran.

During the reign of Herod the Great, members of the Essene priesthood left their home at Qumran and relocated in the Essene Quarter in Jerusalem. Here they dwelled until Herod's death. At that time they moved back to the mountains which overlook the Dead Sea. When Jesus sent John and Peter to prepare the place for his Messianic Banquet he sent them to the Essene Quarter. There they met their contact who led them to the place where they would celebrate their banquet. This Upper Room to which John and Peter were taken had once been used as the refectory by the Essenes during their relocation.[19] It was the dining hall in which they had held their cult meals in preparation and expectation of the Messianic Banquet.

The monastic structure of Qumran is not that of Jesus and his disciples. It is only during the Last Supper where this exclusive practice of a meal is limited to Jesus and the Twelve. In the Messianic Rule, a description is given of the final Messianic Banquet: "And then the Messiah of Israel shall come, and the chiefs of the clans of Israel shall sit before him."

This was the news Judas carried to the Sanhedrin which raised their great alarm. This was Jesus' formal declaration — the first time he openly claimed the role and title of the king-Messiah of Israel! Caiaphas had suspected a rebellion that would come and endanger the whole nation. He believed that this military movement would come from the king-Messiah of the Essenes, Jesus of Nazareth. Now his fears were confirmed, Jesus had performed the one, final act to proclaim himself as king. He had officially accepted his Messiahship.

Caiaphas knew of the Messianic movement when the king-Messiah appeared, an open rebellion would result against the Roman occupation. Not only would this endanger the nation, it would mean an end of the Pharisees' control of the Temple. This caused the Pharisees to repudiate the Messianic movement and the End of Days. The Pharisees expected Jesus to be this military leader so they immediately took action and had him arrested. They moved to squelch this expected military rebellion before it had a chance to begin. "Caiaphas gave counsel to the Jews, that it was expedient that one man should die for the people" (Jn. 18:12-14).[20]

The grounds for the charges brought against Jesus centered on his claim to be the king-Messiah of Israel, a political liberator and messianic conqueror who would destroy the hateful foreign power. It remains historically dubious whether there was a trial of Jesus by the Sanhedrin based on a religious charge. The sentence pronounced by the Sanhedrin was subject to confirmation and execution by Pontius Pilate, the Roman procurator. Only he could authorize the death pen-

159

alty.²¹ But they did not bring a Jewish religious indictment against Jesus, one which could be admissible in a court of the time to be discussed by the Sanhedrin.²² The charge they made against Jesus was the secular charge of treason. They could not charge him with sacrilege of the Temple, but instead accused him of claiming to be the Messiah — the King of Israel. This was the charge they took to Pilate.

Surely Pilate identified Jesus as the object of the Pharisees' hatred. Pilate outwardly hated and despised the Jews. This alone could have been sufficient reason for him to dismiss their demands and to acquit Jesus. "Then said Pilate to the chief priests and to the people, I find no fault in this man" (Lk. 23:4).

But the Jews shouted: "If thou let this man go, thou art not Caesar's friend! Whosoever maketh himself king, speaketh against Caesar" (Jn. 19:12). Passover is the time when Jews remember Pharaoh and confess during the service "we have no King but God." Now, during this Passover, the chief priests cried out to Pilate, "We have no king but Caesar" (Jn. 19:15).

This was a political threat aimed directly at Pilate. Pontius Pilate had brought the golden shields of the emperor to Jerusalem and had hung them in Herod's palace. This was a serious offense to their religious guarantees which had already been granted by Rome. The Jews had appealed to Rome and secured their rights. Emperor Tiberius had ordered the golden shields be removed. Because of this and other arbitrary actions counter to Roman policy, Pilate's standing with Rome at the time of the trial was at a low ebb. The charge against Jesus, "making himself king" implied an act of treason against the Roman emperor. If Pilate dismissed the charges, this would open him to charges by the Jews of neglecting his duties by acquitting a rebel. Pilate feared this threat. He had not forgotten they had carried out their threat before.

Pontius Pilate succumbed but he symbolized his refusal to take responsibility for the death of Jesus by calling for water and washing his hands. Thus Pilate had Jesus bound over to the Roman soldiers to have the death sentence carried out:

"When Pilate therefore heard that saying, he brought Jesus forth, and sat down in the judgment seat, in a place that is called the Pavement, but in the Hebrew, Gabbatha. Then delivered he him therefore unto them to be crucified" (Jn. 19:13-16).

The pavement in Pilate's court where the judgment took place survived the destruction of Jerusalem in A.D. 70. The rediscovery of the pavement was the result of years of work by the archaeologist Father L.H. Vincent. His success was due to the exact description given in the Gospel of St. John. Just inside the northwest perimeter wall of the Temple was the Tower of Antonia. It stood upon this rocky eminence. During the war, the Romans used it as a garrison. In A.D. 70, after the conquest of Jerusalem, Titus had the castle of Antonia destroyed. Later buildings arose upon the ruins. Here Vincent established this large flat pavement of 3,000 square yards built in Roman style during the time of Jesus. This is where Jesus stood before Pilate and it was here he took his scourging in preparation for his crucifixion. He was stripped naked and flogged until his flesh hung down in shreds.

The Jewish court had condemned Jesus as the false Christ, the false king-Messiah of Israel. Pilate referred to Jesus as the "King of the Jews," as did the Roman garrison and the sign that was nailed to the cross above his head. But the priests and scribes mocked Jesus as "the Christ, the King of Israel" (Mk. 15:31-32).

The term "the Jews" serves John, as it did the Essenes as a symbol for all who are God's enemies. Where the Romans and foreigners refer to "Jews" and give Jesus the derisive title "King of the Jews," the Jewish priests themselves use the Essene title, "Messiah, the King of Israel."

Among the thousands of people who were present to witness the crucifixion were those who had first gathered at the Passover three years before to hear the Sermon delivered by the one who had come to save them. At last their wait would culminate in the event in which the Messiah would manifest himself. The long awaited day had finally arrived. Jesus'

161

followers and his disciples expected a tremendous display of power that would overcome the Romans and usher in the new kingdom. Even Judas Iscariot fully expected this to happen. He was present at the crucifixion among the rest of Jesus' followers. He had lived with Jesus, seen his miracles and heard his words. There was no doubt in his mind who Jesus really was. In only a short time the whole world would know.

Jesus was crucified and died on the cross. It caused shock and total disbelief for all who had expected his manifestation. The crowd was left in bewilderment. Belief among his followers was so great in Jesus as Messiah, that when their expectations were not fulfilled, they became totally lost as to their purpose and what their future actions would be.

The result of this unbelievable event was no more astounding to anyone as it was to Judas. Not only was he not going to be one of the most famous heroes in Jewish history, he would also become one of the most infamous people of all time. It was not from the remorse of guilt but rather as a result of desolate disillusionment that Judas later hanged himself.

"After this, Joseph of Arimathea, who was a disciple of Jesus, but secretly for fear of the Jews, asked Pilate that he might take away the body of Jesus, and Pilate gave him leave. So he came and took away his body. Nicodemus also, who had at first come to him at night, came bringing a mixture of myrrh and aloes, about a hundred pounds weight. They took the body of Jesus, and bound it in linen clothes with the spices, as is the burial custom of the Jews. Now in the place where he was crucified there was a garden, and in the garden a new tomb where no one had ever been laid. So because of the Jewish day of Preparation, as the tomb was close at hand, they laid Jesus there" (Jn. 19:38-42).

These events which culminated 200 years of preparation by the Essenes and three years of Jesus' ministry began a new age. His death marked their Day of Atonement. The eschatological clock began ticking.

162

15

The Aftermath

People who lived during the days of the New Testament were filled with anxieties and hopes, doubts and expectations. The Jews lived according to the Law. The Essenes aspired to unyielding strictness. The Pharisees and Sadducees yielded to the compatibility of Greek thought. All Jews were united in the conviction that God had entrusted Israel with the Law to show Israel the intended way of life. The coming of the Messiah was an anticipation of the continuation and heightening of God's Commandment. Even the Messiah would live under the Law.

When Jesus made his way to Jerusalem for the final time, Jerusalem and the Temple were at their greatest period of brilliance. Anyone approaching Jerusalem could see from a distance the elevated Temple which appeared as a bright snow-covered hill. During the reign of Herod the Great, the Temple had been completely restored and its area enlarged to twice its earlier size, secured by the erection of retaining walls. Herod had spared no expense. One proverb states, "Anyone who has not seen Herod's building has not yet seen anything beautiful." When Jesus stood before the Temple with his disciples, they called attention to the greatness of the building, "Master, see what marvelous stones and buildings!" (Mk. 13:2).

The Temple offered an impressive sight to its viewers. Passing through the gates of the city and approaching the Temple, visitors first came upon the outer court, which was open even to Gentiles. The outer court was bordered by a wall with covered colonnades on the inner side traversing the length and width of the entire Temple square. Solomon's porch was located on the east side, and the columned porch was said to have been built by King Solomon (Jn. 10:33).

Pilgrims who traveled great distances to observe the Jewish holy days, could not bring sacrificial animals with them. Unblemished animals were sold in the outer court. Cattle and goats were for sale, and for the poor, doves were sold so they too could offer a small sacrifice. Tyrian coinage was used, and for those who did not have this money, moneychangers had to exchange the coins which the pilgrims brought with them into the coins which were legal tender in the Temple area.

The outer court was closed off from the rest of the Temple area by walls surrounding the Temple. Warning placards were posted stating that anyone found unlawfully inside these walls would be responsible for his own punishment by death. This warning was even heeded by the Roman soldiers, and they avoided trespassing on the sacred precincts. Next to the entrance into the inner court lay many beggars who hoped for charitable contributions. Jewish women were permitted to enter but only into its eastern precincts. This court for women was surrounded by a columned portico. Offering boxes were placed where women could leave gifts for the Temple cultus. The western part of the inner court was reserved for Jewish men because only they could observe the cultus.

In front of the Temple stood the altar of burnt offering. The golden altar of incense, the seven-branched lamp stand, and the table of shewbread where 12 new loaves were placed each Sabbath, stood inside. The Holy of Holies was removed from the rest of the Temple. Only the high priest was allowed to enter on the great Day of Atonement when he performed the expiation of sins for all of Israel. The Holy of Holies had once contained the Ark of the Covenant. It was lost during the destruction of the Temple by the Babylonians. When the Temple was rebuilt, this place was left vacant. From that time on, the blood of the goat which was offered by the high priest for the sins of Israel, instead of being sprinkled on the Ark, was sprinkled on the stone upon which the Ark once stood.

The high priest led the other priests in their service in the Temple. He was the head of the Sanhedrin and ranked highest in the Jewish community. Only he could perform the cultic acts on the great Day of Atonement.

During the major feast days, great throngs of people came to Jerusalem. Often their numbers exceeded the total of the inhabitants who lived in the city. Jerusalem was regarded as the possession of all Israel and its citizens were obliged to provide hospitality to the pilgrims without charge.

The Feast of the Passover was observed in Jerusalem in the spring. It was a time for celebrating the liberation of Israel from captivity in Egypt. The room in which the Passover meal was to be eaten had to be cleansed of everything leavened. When the people fled from Egypt, they had eaten only unleavened bread. An unblemished, year-old male lamb was sacrificed at the Temple, and then prepared according to the prescriptions of the Law.

The Passover meal began with the father speaking over the first cup of wine. The family partook of a relish made of bitter herbs. The meal was then served and a second cup of wine was poured. Before the meal was eaten and the wine drunk, the father performed the Passover liturgy.

The experience of Israel during the time of the exodus from Egypt explains why the Passover foods were eaten. Bitter herbs were served as a reminder of their bitter experience in Egypt. Unleavened bread was eaten because there was no time to wait until the leaven had caused the dough to rise when Israel had to make its hasty departure from Egypt.

A song of praise was raised and then a second cup of wine was drunk. Then the Passover lamb was eaten after a prayer by the father. The feast ended with a prayer over a third cup of wine. At the end of the meal, the second part of the liturgy was recited. Then a praise was lifted in a final pronouncement over a fourth cup which was served.

Fifty days after the Passover came the Feast of Pentecost. The offerings of fruits from the first harvests of the field were brought to Jerusalem and the Temple to give thanks to God for the previous fruitful year. The people also observed the giving of the Law on Mt. Sinai at Pentecost.

The Feast of Tabernacles was celebrated in the autumn. The people went to the altar and thanked God for the harvest.

In addition to these three pilgrim feasts which were celebrated at the Temple in Jerusalem there was also the great Day of Atonement. The importance to the entire nation was the ritual of expiation performed by the high priest. He first sacrificed a goat for the expiation of his own sins and then conferred the sins of Israel upon a second goat.

The Temple, where the sacrifices were offered daily and where thousands of pilgrims journeyed for the great festivals, was the Holy Place for the entire Jewish community. Jerusalem always remained the center of Jewish life, even for the Jews in Diaspora.

With the crucifixion of Jesus in A.D. 26, the Passover ended with his followers returning to their homes and to their former lives without any sense of direction. The movement almost suffered total collapse. But the story of Jesus endured. His disciples believed that God raised him from the dead, and this provided a new foundation for their movement. With the return of Jesus from the dead, he opened their minds to understanding the scriptures. The events that took place during his ministry and his words took on a new meaning. Christians insisted that the highest messianic action was Jesus' death. "Thus it is written that the Christ should suffer and on the third day rise from the dead" (Lk. 24:46).

Christian Jews assembled passages to prove the messianic nature of Jesus' death. They were convinced that the crucified and risen Jesus was truly the Messiah and developed a very different doctrine from the traditional messianic beliefs. The Gospels redefined for their readers the true messiahship in the

166

light of Jesus' death.

John's Gospel may have been written first because the responsibility rested upon the highest ranking among the disciples or it may have been because he had the greatest formal training among the disciples in Essaeic thought. His work interprets the ministry of Jesus in light of the Old Testament and Qumran passages. It is aimed to influence the Essene community and its priesthood that their long awaited promises and the traditional messianic texts had been fulfilled. Jesus "reigns from the tree;" his crucifixion is a "lifting up" — an exaltation. Jesus is not an executed martyr; he is the crucified Messiah! He was sent by God as the Messiah, and was God's chosen expositor of the Law. Those who share in God's covenant — God's chosen people — are believers in Jesus Christ.

For the Essene priesthood, one's relationship with God is determined by the Law. To speak of God is to speak of His Law. This is the way that God's Will is made manifest. One seeks righteousness through the Law and there is no other way to salvation. God has made His Will known in the Word and there is no other source of revelation. The Messiah is a king. He will appear as a ruler and exalt the lowliness of Israel, drive out the heathen and establish his Kingdom of Glory. He will rule over Israel and all nations. There could not be a suffering messiah to take the guilt of others upon himself.

There was never an issue as to the miracles which Jesus performed — his healing of the sick, feeding the multitudes or raising of the dead. Even his own resurrection was not contested. Many miraculous deeds were entrenched in the history of Israel and the events of the great men of God. Members of the priesthood were conservative in their opinion of Jesus' miracles; they did not doubt the possibility or the actuality of them. The priesthood and its followers had witnessed many of his miracles, but they had never recognized them as any definitive proof in settling messianic claims. The awaited Messianic Age would be filled with God's miraculous activities but the priesthood did not conceive of the Messiah as a miracle worker. He would demonstrate his power by the fulfillment of scripture.

The movement of Jesus' followers did not end when he returned to heaven. They first recruited and converted those within their own Community. The first group of followers met in the Upper Room, the Essene sanctuary in Jerusalem. There they were commissioned to preach "repentance and forgiveness of sins...to all nations, beginning in Jerusalem" (Lk. 24:47). Jesus promised that they would "receive power when the Holy Spirit has come upon you; and you shall be my witnesses in Jerusalem and in all Judea and Samaria and to the end of the earth" (Acts 1:8).

Paul, the Pharisee who was converted from a fierce opponent to one of Jesus' greatest ministers, was such a dynamic force in the movement that Luke devoted nearly half of the Book of Acts to him.[1] The great missionary presented the Word to the Gentile world and even carried it to Rome where he was martyred by Emperor Nero. Followers converted the first non-Jews into their movement. The Word reached the ends of the earth, or more appropriately, to the center of the earth.

The first speech in the Acts of the Apostles is the sermon presented by Peter at Pentecost. Those who gathered to hear him were devout Jews who came from every nation. He spoke to these "men of Judea" and "men of Israel" about a prophecy of the "last days" that had been fulfilled — a new age in the history of Israel had arrived.

Peter quoted passages from Psalms 16, 132 and 110 that identify Jesus as the resurrected Christ and as the second Lord. Peter urged that those who are baptized in the name of Jesus Christ receive the gift of forgiveness. Peter converted 3,000 Jews and this began a new era in Israel as foretold by the scriptures. These converts had not broken from Jewish tradition and continued their daily worship in the Temple.

Later Peter and John healed the sick in the Temple in the name of Jesus. Peter again told the Jews that God had fulfilled His promises "foretold by the mouth of all the prophets,"

168

that Jesus' death and resurrection marked the beginning of a time of crisis. Peter quoted Moses from Deuteronomy 18:18-19, which clearly describes the crisis:

"Moses said, 'The Lord God will raise up for you a prophet from your brethren as he raised me up. You shall listen to him in whatever he tells you. And it shall be that every soul that does not listen to that prophet shall be destroyed from the people.' And all the prophets who have spoken, from Samuel and those who came afterwards, also proclaimed these days. You are sons of the prophets and of the covenant which God gave to your fathers, saying to Abraham, 'And in your posterity shall all the families of the earth be blessed.' God having raised up His servant, sent him to you first, to bless you in turning every one of you from your wickedness" (Acts 3:22-26).

The coming of Jesus is significant for what it says about the fulfillment of scripture and for what it means for Israel. The coming of the "prophet like Moses" will signal a time of crisis. Membership into the nation of Israel will depend on the response of each person to his teaching. Those who do not heed the words of the "prophet like Moses" will be rooted out, forfeiting their right to be called Jews.

Only those who believe in Jesus are true Jews. Peter did not propose a movement of a new religious sect. Instead, he viewed the movement as a purge foretold in scripture within the Jewish community and the formation of a new remnant. The followers of Jesus are pious Jews. The story of Jesus is the story of Israel, the story of Jerusalem, with references to the fulfillment of the patriarchal promises. The life of Jesus is part of a whole history that began with Abraham and extends into the future. It is a tale of a religious community that will carry the message to the end of the earth. The life of Jesus is an episode in a story that has an earlier, as well as a later, stage; his life is not related to the world nor to the Roman Empire, but rather to the nation of Israel. These days following Christs' resurrection represent the latest and most decisive stage in the story of Israel. The coming of the Messiah signals a winnowing out among Jews. The God who raised Jesus is the same God of Abraham, Isaac and Jacob. He is the God of the New Covenant that continues.

Many Jews continued to reject the claims of Jesus' followers. Opponents included Jewish officials who controlled the Temple, the most influential members of the Jewish community and leaders of the people. The opposition that Jesus faced also continued against the early church. Peter and John were arrested. Stephen was stoned. Paul was persecuted wherever he went. Paul was finally arrested in Jerusalem but managed a miraculous escape avoiding death at the hands of a Jewish mob. In the case of Paul, like that of Jesus, the Roman authorities testified that he had committed no crime against Roman law. The opposition and division existed only within the Jewish community.

When Caesar Augustus died in A.D. 14, his adopted son Tiberius took over the Roman government. During his reign the orderly succession and administration of the empire continued. Tiberius installed Pontius Pilate as procurator in Judea and Samaria. Jesus pursued his work until A.D. 26 when the Jews handed him over to the governor in Jerusalem.

Caligula took over the rule of Tiberius in A.D. 37. Caligula surrounded himself with corrupt Hellenistic princes, one of whom was Herod Agrippa who managed to gain influence and rule in Palestine through Caligula's favor. Caligula strove for godlike exaltation. He even demanded that the Jews set up his statue likeness in the Temple in Jerusalem. He made so many enemies during his rule that a palace revolution ended his regime.

For a brief period, Palestine again came under the rule of a Jewish king. The grandson of King Herod, Agrippa was given rule over the territory that Philip had once ruled and two years later he gained the land of the exiled Herod Antipas. In A.D. 41 he was also given rule over Judea, Samaria and Idumea. Under his rule, the entire kingdom his grandfather had ruled was reunited.

Herod Agrippa presented himself as a devoted Jew who was concerned with the Law. To the Hellenistic population he appeared as a Hellenistic prince who sought to enhance his image by erecting numerous buildings. He managed to control the Pharisees, persecute the Christian community, have St. John's brother James executed, have Peter thrown into prison and have himself hailed as a divinely-sent Hellenistic prince. When he died, the entire country was annexed to Syria and controlled by Roman procurators.

Years later, Agrippa II received control over the territory which Philip had once ruled. He also oversaw the Temple in Jerusalem where he caused offense and created friction by making appointments to the office of high priest at his whim.

In A.D. 41 to 54, Claudius, the uncle of Caligula, became Caesar. Although he was a reasonable man and governed conscientiously, Claudius took steps against the Jews in Rome. Under his rule, the Jews were expelled from the city because of the continued unrest which resulted from the spread of the message of Christ among the Jews. The proclamation that Jesus of Nazareth was the Messiah of Israel caused the outbreak of these disturbances which Claudius understood as justification to expel all Jews from the city.

In A.D. 52 Felix received favor of Emperor Claudius and became Roman procurator of Palestine. Felix maintained the royal law by acts of cruelty and greed. Hate against the Roman occupation in Palestine continued to escalate. Zealots wanted to use force to throw off the foreign yoke and they found growing support among those who felt tormented by the malicious conduct of the Romans.

In A.D. 54 Claudius was poisoned by his wife Agrippina who wanted her son Nero, who was born of her first marriage, brought to the throne. The change of power was made without upheaval. The first persecution of Christians in Rome arose at Nero's instigation. After the fire in Rome in A.D. 64, the rumor spread that Nero had been responsible for having the fire set. To divert suspicion from himself, he shifted the blame to the Christians and condemned those to death whose property people coveted. Nero even murdered members of his own family. Things became so unbearable that by A.D. 68 a conspiracy was organized against him and Nero took his own life.

In Palestine, Felix was replaced about A.D. 60 by Porcius Festus. Although he was a man who followed the Law, tensions between Jews and Romans did not lessen. Festus had Paul arrested and sent him to Rome where he was tried and sentenced. The reign of Festus ended with his death in A.D. 62.

The Roman occupation forces caused the Jewish people's hatred to grow. Protests against the empire continued. Zealots banded together and demanded the removal of the foreign power. Their violent deeds created unrest, and more supporters joined with the radicals.

The Essene priesthood did not believe Jesus to be the Messiah.[2] They believed the Messiah would come at the End of Days when the House of Zadok would be returned to the Temple. The priesthood did believe that Jesus played an important role in their scriptures. He was born under the star, a descendent of David, and within their own Community. One of their own priests, John the Baptist, had recognized him and christened him. They had watched as he performed great feats. They recorded his words. No one had ever spoken as this man. He gave the crowds manna as Moses once did and he accepted his messiahship at his Messianic Banquet.

The 53rd chapter of Isaiah tells of "a man of sorrows, and aquainted with grief...despised and rejected of men...but he was wounded for our transgressions...by his knowledge shall my Righteous Servant justify many; for he shall bear their iniquities." Christians believe this to be a direct prophecy, a prediction of the advent, suffering and death of Jesus, who is referred to as "the Man of Sorrows" from this very passage.

The Essene priesthood placed great importance on Isaiah and it was revered very highly in their canon. They believed that the 53rd chapter of Isaiah referred to their own beloved Teacher of Righteousness, especially the verse that refers to "my Righteous Servant," which is even more closely worded in the Revised Standard Version of Isaiah: "by his knowledge shall the Righteous Teacher, my servant, make many to be

172

accounted righteous; and he shall bear their iniquities." Jesus, "the Suffering Servant" was asserted by the Essenes to be their Master, their Righteous Teacher.

God chose to reveal His purpose through knowledge and understanding of their Righteous Teacher. Only the Teacher could decipher the mysteries concealed in the Scriptures. The End of Days was at hand and the prophecies alluding to these final days referred to the Community of the Covenant. "All those who observe the Law in the House of Judah...God will deliver from the House of Judgment because of their suffering and because of their faith in the Teacher of Righteousness" (QHAB II:14).

Members of the Essene priesthood recognized the reincarnation of their Righteous Teacher in Jesus. They regarded him as the embodiment of a divine teacher who had often reappeared on earth. When Jesus sent John and Peter to Jerusalem to prepare the Messianic Banquet, he instructed them to say, "The *Teacher* says, 'Where is my guest room?' " (Mk. 14:14).

The priesthood believed the coming of the Messiah would be preceded by an age of trial and tribulation. Satan would try his utmost to lead the chosen astray. According to CD II, the Messianic Age would begin 40 years after the death of the Teacher of Righteousness. In the Messianic Rule I, the priests expected a large-scale conversion to the Community on the eve of the new age. After that last moment, according to the Damascus Document IV, there would be "no more joining the House of Judah." All of the elect would then be under the Prince of Light, and the rest of mankind — Jews and Gentiles alike — would be committed to the Sons of Darkness under the Angel of Darkness.

According to their War Rule, 40 years of terrible fighting would ensue until all the wickedness would be wiped away from the earth and truth and goodness would reign forever. The elect would inherit the "glory of Adam...every blessing and eternal joy of life without end, a crown of glory and a garment of majesty in unending light" (QS IV).

173

The priests expected to remain in exile until they would reoccupy Jerusalem and conquer the world by defeating the Gentiles and the king of the Roman Empire. "The sons of Levi, Judah, and Benjamin, the exiles in the desert, shall battle against them in all their bands when the exiled Sons of Light return from the Desert of the People to camp in the Desert of Jerusalem; and after the battle they shall go up from there to Jerusalem" (QM V).

The undercurrent of anti-Roman sentiment and the Zealot movement were instructed to wait for the proper time. The priests were convinced that Jesus was the one sent to prepare them for the final days and the Zealot movement would join on the side of God to carry out His will at the prescribed time. By waiting and joining the Essene movement, God Himself would underwrite their success.

In the War Rule, military preparation would begin seven years before the final war was to begin. The Essene community was completely dedicated to the military preparation that would culminate in eternal redemption. This military preparation for war was evident to the Christians living within the Essene community. The Zealots came into the movement; they only had to await the proper moment.

John writes in his final work a warning to the Essene priesthood using their own symbolism and imagery: "Blessed is he who listens to the words of this prophetic message and obeys what is written in this book! For the time is near when all this will happen" (Rev. 1:3).

The fortieth anniversary of the death of Jesus marked the Essene Day of Vengeance. The final battle would commence during the sixth month of the sixty-sixth year.[3] The enemy would move from the north with a tremendous force never seen before. Everything in its path would be laid in ruins. "This calls for wisdom: let him who has understanding reckon the number of the beast, for it is a human number, its number is six hundred and sixty-six" (Rev. 13:18).

The brutal conduct of the Romans continued. And they offered no protection from anti-Jewish demonstrations which arose in Caesarea among the Hellenistic inhabitants. In A.D. 66 Gessius Florus stole 17 talents from the Temple. He also allowed his troops to plunder the city. Florus advanced more troops to Jerusalem and demanded that the Jews welcome them with ceremony; the high priest and the Pharisees advised the people to yield to his demand. The people submitted to this profound humiliation.

On the Day of Vengeance, the Zealots, who had waited for the proper time, were led by John of Gischala[4] quickly into Jerusalem and occupied the Temple area. This revolt was not spontaneous, but a well orchestrated raid carried out by a trained and armed military strike force. It infiltrated Jerusalem and overcame the Roman occupation troops so quickly and effectively that the Romans didn't know what was happening until it was too late. The governor was forced to retreat back to Caesarea leaving behind one legion stranded in the fortified citadel of Antonia.

Agrippa tried to persuade the Jews that resistance to Rome was sheer madness. The high priest, the chief priests and the Pharisees all called for moderation. But their call went unheeded and the daily sacrifice offered to Caesar was discontinued. Those Jews suspected of not being in the camp of the Sons of Light were slain. The high priest who had tried to prevent the uprising was murdered; others were forced to join the movement.

The prohibition of daily sacrifices to the Roman emperor meant an open declaration of war. The occupation forces had been taken by surprise and no longer had control of the situation. Syria's governor, C. Cestius Gallus, marched to Jerusalem to rescue the legion stranded in the citadel. Antonia was overrun by the Zealots and the entire city fell into the hands of the Jews. Gallus had to retreat with heavy losses and the rebels controlled all of Palestine.

Aware that the empire would strike back, the rebels hastened to fortify the cities. Old defense walls were repaired. Among the commanders appointed was Josephus, who had completed one year of initiation into the Essene church. He was sent from Jerusalem as Commander-In-Chief of Galilee to lead a task force in preparation of fortifications in the northern part of the country.

Emperor Nero chose General Titus Vespasianus as commander. Vespasian was a brilliant soldier who had distinguished himself in the conquest of Britain. Accompanied by his son Titus, he advanced on Galilee from the north with three of the best legions in the army and numerous auxiliaries. As the army advanced, the Jews panicked and retreated into fortresses. All of Galilee came under the Romans without a struggle. Josephus and his people managed to hold out in a 47 day siege in Jotapota. When their resistance collapsed, the Essene Zealots demanded that the rebels commit suicide by taking poison.

Josephus rejected this demand and surrendered to Vespasian. He was led away in chains to Vespasian's headquarters. From there he saw the rest of the Jewish war from the enemy's camp and later gave his eyewitness account of the history of the entire Jewish War. John of Gischala escaped and returned to Jerusalem with a small band. Six thousand Jews were enslaved and sent to work on the Corinth Canal. Once again Galilee was in the hands of the Romans.

The suppression of the rebels did not continue until the following spring. John of Gischala became the leader of the Zealots in Jerusalem and he seized the Temple. The forces under Simon bar Giora occupied the rest of Jerusalem. Open warfare broke out between the conservatives and the followers of the Essene movement. Meanwhile, the Romans patiently waited and watched the developments in Jerusalem.

Vespasian learned from his captives the priesthood at Qumran was responsible for the ideology behind this revolt against Rome. In the spring, the Romans marched down the Jordan Valley into Judea. The Zealots offered a short resistance and then retreated. As a prelude to the forthcoming attack on Jerusalem, the monastery at Qumran was captured and the priests and scribes were taken as prisoners.

Vespasian tested the strange stories of the buoyancy of the

Dead Sea by throwing his captives into it with their hands tied behind their backs. The priests did not resist their demise for they believed it to be the final act before the coming of the new kingdom and the End of Days.

"And as for death, if it will be for their glory, they esteem it better than living always; and indeed our war with the Romans gave abundant evidence what great souls they had in their trials, wherein, although they were tortured and distorted, burnt and torn to pieces, and went through all kinds of instruments of torment, that they might be forced either to blaspheme their legislator, or to eat what was forbidden them, yet could they not be made to do either of them, no, nor once to flatter their tormentors, or to shed a tear; but they smiled in their very pains, and laughed those to scorn who inflicted the torments upon them, and resigned up their souls with great alacrity, as expecting to receive them again.

"For their doctrine is this: That bodies are corruptible, and that the matter they are made of is not permanent; but that the souls are immortal, and continue forever; and that they come out of the most subtile air, and are united to their bodies as in prisons, into which they are drawn by a certain natural enticement; but that when they are set free the bonds of the flesh, they then, as released from a long bondage, rejoice and mount upward" (Josephus — The Jewish War).

In the midst of the fighting, news came that Nero had committed suicide. The campaign was temporarily halted. Civil war broke out in Rome. One after another three succeeding emperors lost their lives. The legions of the east finally stepped in and called Vespasian to become emperor. Vespasian became the master of the Roman Empire. He received word in Caesarea and departed for Rome, leaving his son Titus to finish the final act in the Jewish War.

Shortly before the full moon in the spring of A.D. 70 during the time of the Passover, the city was swarming with pilgrims from all over the world. The war continued between the Zealots and the moderates. The wounded and dead were left unattended. Titus marched on Jerusalem with four legions and numerous auxiliary forces to surround the city trapping its inhabitants and the pilgrims. Marching columns filled the roads leading to Jerusalem. The 5th, 10th, 12th and 15th legions made up the army accompanied by the cavalry, engineers and other auxiliary troops totaling 80,000 men. The Roman camps were moved into the outskirts of Jerusalem. With the deaths of the Essene priests and scribes, Titus now believed the backbone of the resistance to be broken. But, surprisingly, his call for the Jews to surrender was met with laughter.

Jerusalem is situated on an elevation and an approach on level ground is only possible from the north. Titus commanded the attack to begin from this direction. Battering rams and siege engines cracked with thunder as they attacked the foundations of the massive walls. Day after day, night and day, the heavy thud of the battering rams could be heard. A constant hail of great stones was hurtled into the city.

Finally, the war within the walls came to an end. Simon bar Giora and the moderates took defense of the north wall. John of Gischala and the Zealots took defense of the Temple and the Tower of Antonia. Two weeks after it had begun, the siege had torn gaping holes into the northern wall. Five days later the Romans had advanced through the second wall. The Jews counterattacked and pushed the Romans back. It took several more days before they could recapture the wall — now the Romans controlled the entire northern suburb.

Titus was so convinced that the Jews would now surrender, that he called off the attack. A grandiose parade marched directly beneath the eyes of the beleaguered people. Titus believed this would surely bring them to their senses. In front of the walls of Jerusalem, tens of thousands of unbeaten warriors marched past Titus and received their pay from early morning until dusk for four days. The trumpets sounded as the cavalry rode by on horseback, the army marched with their highly polished coats of mail and helmets. The old wall was packed tight with people who spat hatred upon the Romans. They had never considered surrender. Titus made one last attempt to end the holdout. He sent Josephus to appeal to them.

"O hard hearted men, throw away your weapons, have pity on your country that stands on the edge of the abyss. Look round and behold the beauty of all that you are ready to betray. What a city. What a Temple! What gifts for so many nations! Who would dare to let all this be given to the flames? Is there one of you who can wish for all this to be more? What more precious treasure could have been given to man to preserve. You obdurate creatures, more unfeeling than these very stones!" (Josephus – The Jewish War).

Josphus' pleas fell on deaf ears. The battle began again from the second wall and surged against Antonia. Another front was pushed to the Temple area in the upper part of the city. The Romans tried every means of siege warfare. The defenders made valiant raids to upset them. At night the Roman camp was crawling with ghostly figures setting fires to the wooden machines and foraging for food. They came out of their hiding places, scaled the walls or crept through the subterranean passages.

Titus ordered reprisals. Anyone caught outside the walls was crucified. Everyday 500 Jews were nailed to crosses overlooking the city. The trees were used for crosses, siege ramps, scaling ladders and campfires. The countryside was flourishing when the Romans had first arrived. Now all was barren. The trees had disappeared. Even the Mount of Olives had vanished. With the lack of wood, Titus called a halt to the crucifixions. A stench rose over the countryside. Bodies of those fallen in battle and those dead of starvation were piled at the foot of the walls.

"No stranger who had seen Judea of old, and the lovely suburbs of its capital, and now saw this devastation could have restrained his tears and lamentations at the hideous change. For the war had turned all that beauty into a wilderness. And no man who knew these places of old and suddenly saw them again could possibly have recognized them" (Josephus — The Jewish War).

In order to stop the smuggling of supplies and provisions into the city, the circumvallatio was erected. It consisted of a wall of earthwork which surrounded the entire city. It was guarded at 13 points and resulted in the smallest, most meager reinforcement being stopped. Death mowed down the overflowing pilgrims as famine haunted the city.

"The terrible famine that increased in frightfulness daily annihilated whole families of the people. The terraces were full of women and children who had collapsed from hunger, the alleys were piled high with the bodies of the aged. Children and young people, swollen with lack of food, wandered around like ghosts until they fell. They were so far spent that they could no longer bury anyone, and if they did they fell dead upon the very corpses they were burying. The misery was unspeakable. For as soon as even the shadow of anything eatable appeared anywhere, a fight began over it, and the best of friends fought each other and tore from each other the most miserable trifles. No one would believe that the dying had no provisions stowed away. Robbers threw themselves upon those who were drawing their last breath and ransacked their clothing. These robbers ran about reeling and staggering like mad dogs and hammered on the doors of houses like drunk men. In their despair they often plunged into the same house two or three times in one day. Their hunger was so unbearable that they were forced to chew anything and everything. They laid hands on things that even the meanest of animals would not touch, far less eat. They had long since eaten their belts and shoes and even their leather jerkins were torn to shreds and chewed. Many of them fed on old hay and there were some who collected stalks of corn and sold a small quantity of it for four Attic drachmas. But why should I describe the shame and indignity that famine brought upon men, making them eat such unnatural things?

"Because I tell of things unknown to history, whether Greek or barbarian. It is frightful to speak of it and unbelievable to hear of it. I should gladly have passed over this disaster in silence, so that I might not get the reputation of recording something which must appear to posterity wholly degrading. But there were too many eyewitnesses in my time. Apart from that my country would have little cause to be grateful to me were I to be silent about the misery which it endured at this time" (Josephus — The Jewish War).

Famine clouded the brains of the blockaded citizens. Many fled the death of starvation and ran right into the arms of the Romans. Rumors spread that the fugitives had swallowed gold and jewels in hopes of preserving them from being seized by the Roman army. Unsuspecting Jews were captured and their bodies slit open in the quest for plunder. In one night alone, 2,000 Jews were killed this way.

Titus was furious. He ordered the cavalry to execute one entire auxiliary unit in an attempt to stop this practice. He issued an order that made the practice a crime punishable by death. The slaughter continued in secret.

Titus grew impatient. He wanted to end the nightmare as quickly as possible. The hammering of the battering rams was stepped up. New ramps were made. In July his soldiers stormed the Tower of Antonia and the castle where Jesus had been sentenced to death was razed to the ground. He then focused his forces on the Temple. His officers wanted to treat the fortified complex of galleries and forecourts as a fortress but Titus opposed this. If at all possible, he wanted to preserve the sanctuary which was known throughout the empire. One last time his heralds demanded that the rebels surrender the Temple.

The Zealots who believed in the End of Days held fast. They held the reigns in their hands and demanded their followers resist the Roman offer with inexorable strictness. They indulged in the hope that in the final hour God would intervene to save the True Remnant. Surely God would not abandon His Holy Place, even if the outer court should be lost and the city and forecourt trampled by the forces of evil:

"Then I was given a measuring rod like a staff, and I was told: 'Rise and measure the Temple of God and the altar and

181

those who worship there, but do not measure the court outside the temple; leave that out, for it is given over to the city for forty-two months' " (Rev. 11:1-2).

"And He built them a sure house in Israel whose like has never existed from former times till now. Those who hold fast to it are destined to live forever and all the glory of Adam shall be theirs" (CD III).

Titus embarked upon the final attack against the holy precincts. Showers of arrows and heavy stones rained down upon the courtyard. The Zealots fought like men possessed. They relied on Yahweh to rescue them at the last possible moment. Each time the legionaries reached the perimeter wall they were thrown back. It was impossible to shatter the vast stone walls Herod had built.

Titus ordered the Temple gates be torched but he wanted to spare the sanctuary. By that night, the fire still raged out of control. It had burned its way into the inner court and the army had its hands full trying to put it out. The Zealots used the distraction as an opportunity to launch a counteroffensive. Their violent attack was met with a remorseless slaughter as the Romans drove the Jews back and pursued them through the courts to the very walls of the sanctuary.

"One of the soldiers, without waiting for orders and without any sense of the horror of his deed, or rather being driven by some evil spirit, seized a blazing torch and, hoisted on the shoulders of one of his comrades, flung it through the Golden Window that opened into the rooms which lay beside the Holy of Holies. The room contained bottles of holy oil and inflammable materials used for sacrifices. The old wood paneling on the walls provided ample fodder for instantaneous combustion.

"Caesar [Titus became Caesar in A.D. 79] then commanded that the fire should be put out, calling in a loud voice to the soldiers who were in the thick of the fighting and given them a signal with his right hand. But they did not hear what he said for all his shouting...and since Caesar was unable to restrain

182

the hot rage of the soldiery, and since the flames were spreading further and further, he entered the Holy Place in the Temple together with his commander and viewed it and all its contents...but since the flames had not yet reached the inner rooms, and were still devouring the rooms that surrounded the Tabernacle, Titus, assuming, as was indeed the case, that the Tabernacle itself could still be saved, hurried away and made every effort to get the soldiers to put out the fire, giving orders to Liberalius, the centurion, and to one of his own bodyguards, to beat the soldiers with staves if they refused and by every means to restrain them. But however great their enthusiasm for Caesar and their dread of what he had forbidden them to do, their hatred of the Jews and their eagerness to fight them was equally great.

"In addition the hope of booty spurred many of them on. They had the impression that all these rooms within were full of gold, and they saw that all around them was made of pure gold...Thus the Holy Place was burnt down without Caesar's approbation.

"Caesar ordered the whole city and the Temple be razed to the ground. He left standing only the towers of Phasael, Hippicus, and Marianne and part of the city wall on the west side. This was to provide quarters for the garrison that was to remain behind" (Josephus — The Jewish War).

The hand of destiny had erased any role that Israel had played in the world of nations. The Jewish loss of life had been high. According to Tacitus, there were 600,000 people in the city during the siege. Josephus accounts for 97,000 Jews taken as prisoners, not counting those who had been ripped open or crucified. During a three-month period, 115,800 Jewish corpses were carried out of one of the city gates alone.

In A.D. 71 Titus paraded his great victory over Jerusalem through the streets of Rome. Along with the 700 other Jewish prisoners in the triumphal procession marched John of Gischala and Simon bar Giora in chains. Two other important trophies were also displayed in the procession to the great joy and rejoicing of the crowds: the Seven-branched candlestick and the Table of the Shewbread taken from the Temple in Jerusalem. Each was to be placed in the Temple of Peace in Rome.

Small groups of rebels persisted in resisting the empire. They were finally driven along the Dead Sea to Masada where they made their final stand. A fortress had been built on a high mountain by King Herod. Here the Zealots were able to make one final stand in the hope that God would not abandon them. The Romans surrounded the mountain and began a siege of the fortress. When it was determined the situation was hopeless, the Zealots committed suicide by taking poison. Only two women and five children managed to hide themselves in an underground water conduit and survive the defense. The Romans entered and found the dead bodies.

The Masada ruins were excavated between 1963 and 1965 by Professor Yigael Yadin. Among some of the documents discovered was a fragment of a scroll entitled the "Angelic Liturgy," an Essaeic document belonging to the Dead Sea Scrolls literature.[5]

With the fall of Masada, the last resistance was broken. Vespasian ordered that Judea be separated from Syria and made it an imperial province. The Tenth Roman Legion was stationed in the country. Synagogues throughout Palestine were razed to the ground, even the synagogue in Capernaum.

With the fall of the Temple, Judaism lost its visible center. The Sadducean movement, which depended on the Temple, was also lost. But the Pharisees were able to continue, due to their foundation of synagogues throughout the world. They stimulated the reconstruction of the Jewish communities which gathered together after the devastating war and they conferred their influential mark upon them.[6]

For the followers of the Essene movement, the end of the war meant they would no longer have the leadership of their priesthood. Everyone of their priests had been killed by Vespasion when he swept down from Galilee as he marched toward Jerusalem. With the fall of the Temple, the sacrificial cultus had also fallen. The worship of God continued in the

184

synagogues and the Temple liturgy was incorporated. A seven-branched lamp stand was set up as had originally stood in the Temple. Prayer was offered with the same regularity as it had been in the Temple and the people besought God to restore the Temple.

The Essene synagogues and those of the Pharisees in the Diaspora were merged into a common tenet. The once opposing doctrines joined to form a new doctrine. The Pharisees, who had once opposed the belief in the End of Days and the eschatological hope for a king-Messiah, now accepted it. Nothing short of a miracle of God would ever return them to Jerusalem and the power and position that had once been theirs.

These two groups were also impelled to merge because of a common enemy. The despised Nazarenes continued to hold revivals in the synagogues as they tried to convince the Jews that the Messiah had already come as Jesus Christ. But those who had believed Jesus to be the Messiah now felt betrayed, for they had counted on his return after the 40 years.

The worship service which the Pharisees installed has remained unchanged to the present. The content of the service consists of two parts: the first has a strong liturgical stamp and the second part consists of instructions. The instructional part of the service is composed of readings and teachings from the important works of the Old Testament. A definitive order of readings was planned for the entire year.

The first part begins with the Shema (meaning "Hear") which is a confession of the one God of Israel, consisting of three passages recited morning and evening. The Shema is then followed by a work called the Eighteen Benedictions. The Benedictions existed during the time of Jesus but they were expanded and enlarged after the war.

The first three and last three Benedictions call on people to praise God. The 12 petitions which make up the main part of the prayer are related to everyday needs and the hope that God will bring about the Messianic Age.

After the war, the Twelfth Benediction was expanded to include the following wording:

"May there be no hope for the apostates, and mayest thou speedily uproot the insolent government [Rome] in our days. And may the Nazarenes [Jewish Christians] and the Minim [Jewish heretics] die in a moment, may they be blotted out of the book of life and not be enrolled with the righteous. Praised be thou, Lord, who doest humble insolence."

This curse was pronounced every day against the Christians and they were excluded from all Jewish services, banned from all Jewish communities and were forbidden to enter any of the synagogues.[7]

The Thirteenth Benediction includes a petition for the eschatological event to be brought about:

"Have pity, O Lord our God, in thy great mercy, upon Israel, thy people, and upon Jerusalem, thy city, and upon Zion, the dwelling place of thy glory, and upon thy temple and upon thy dwelling and upon thy kingdom of the house of David, of thy righteous Messiah. Praised be thou, Lord, God of David, who dost build up Jerusalem."

Paul had preached that the story of Jesus and his work were part of a scheme of redemptive history stretching back to Moses, Abraham, Isaac and Jacob. He used Israel's past to legitimize the Christian claims about Jesus, and to exhort, censure or edify the Christian communities, as well as to illustrate a point or to convince an opponent in an argument. Early Christians believed that Jesus would soon return to put an end to all of history. Most of them could remember the time when Jesus was alive. Although his death had thrown them into confusion, in his resurrection they saw a sign that the final countdown of history had begun. But the Lord had not returned. Those who had expected to see his coming had now died. This first generation of Christians had been convinced it would see the Lord's return; second and third generations had to modify these expectations. The future grew more and more remote and it no longer brimmed with promise.

Although Christianity began to flourish, there was no End of Days. By the end of the first century, the Christians only numbered a few thousand. This Christian community could

186

not be easily distinguished from Jewish communities. Decade after decade, the Lord did not come. Imperceptibly, Christianity was becoming part of a historical process. It began to fix standards of behavior, shape a system of beliefs, establish patterns of organization for its communities and regulate the cultus. Followers began to realize that the magical moment had passed. The generation which had known the Lord was dying and another was taking its place.

Luke writes of a new situation he found at the close of the first century. Members of the Community had gathered in expectation of the End of Days, but the Lord had not returned. They now had to view themselves in the light of other men, other experiences, other ways of life and other beliefs. Many still believed Jesus had spoken the truth, that he had risen from the dead, that he was present with them always and that he was worthy of their trust.

The Book of Acts records the events of the first four decades which followed the resurrection, but it reflects the viewpoint of a Christian who lived a full generation later. Christians had to explain to themselves and to others why there was now a "time" of the church between the death of Jesus and the End of Days. Christianity, according to Luke, is not the revelation of God through Jesus to be followed by the end of the world. There would be a period of time, a span of years, between his resurection and his return. During this period the church would face crises, growth, conflicts, expansion and setbacks. Luke's book has no end; it concludes midstream as if the tale may continue indefinitely.

When Luke looked at the church, the past was quickly slipping into oblivion. Those who had known Jesus were now gone and new leaders were rising. Because the spread of Christianity made it difficult to insure the traditions of Jesus would be kept intact, Luke believed that the church needed reliable guarantees of its proclamation. The most reliable witnesses were those of the first generation of followers who had lived with Jesus. Among these eyewitnesses, Luke notes that members of the apostolic band in particular could be counted on as reliable sources. They not only saw the works and heard the words of the Father through Jesus, they received the gift of apostolic authority in the way of the Spirit after his ascension. The apostles became the sole trustworthy witnesses to the origin of the faith; they became the Christian consciousness.

First there was Israel, the patriarchs, Moses and the prophets. Then came Jesus, his resurrection and ascension, the beginning of the Christian faith and now the time of the church. Luke passed on the barest outline of a construction of the past suitable to a new community in the new situation it found itself. The expectations of the first generation now gave way to the belief of the second and third generations that Jesus would not come back at any moment. The church no longer existed solely in anticipation of the End of Days. Instead, it became immersed in a history of its own, with memories of its heroes and former days, and a sense that it would continue for some time until the Lord would come. This was now the time of the church. Past, present and future stretched from the beginning of the world until the day when Jesus would return.

16

One Final Word

The Roman Empire attained the height of its power and prosperity during the first half of the second century. It stretched from northern Britain to the Euphrates, from the Rhine and the Danube to the Atlas Mountains. Conquests fed the buoyant economy. The stable and self-confident society lived in a cosmopolitan culture. The empire had achieved its greatest extent.

Christianity began within the unity provided by the Jewish religion of its first proponents. Pentecost had for a time reversed the trend toward evolution and it could be seen that the destiny of the church was to expand and grow in the image and unity of Christ. The character of the Community derived strength from its narrowness. It sprang from the faithful observance of the Law of Moses and the close fellowship of a common life centered around Jesus. But this character lasted only a brief time as the message was carried into wider circles. The challenge was to practice principles of unity when the structure in which the message spread was no longer comparable to the structure in which it was received.

During the second century, growth began to bring Christianity out of the shadows. Its strength lay in the eastern provinces of the Roman Empire, with only a few churches existing in the west. Rome, as the center of the world, naturally became the center of importance. The destruction of Jerusalem created a vacuum for those Judeo-Christians who looked toward it for religious reasons and the capital of the empire now conveniently took its place. The martyrdoms of St. Peter and St. Paul in Rome added to its importance. Although Rome became known as the center of Christianity, it was not because of the city's proximity to the largest number of Christian communities, for it was, in fact, a considerable distance from them. It was because all communications went through Rome.

As the church spread and the apostles died or were martyred, another system of authority had to be established. There was no agreement as to the coming of the Messiah, but clearly it might not be in the immediate future. Long-term arrangements necessitated a recognized form of authority. The first signs of differing beliefs appeared, a prelude to what would become a growing problem throughout the subsequent centuries.

Organization within local churches began with the establishment of presbyters (elders) who were the leaders of the communities. In larger towns and cities where more than one was needed, one of the presbyters was elevated to the position of bishop, which means "overseer" or "supervisor," over all the rest.[1] By the start of the second century, the office had more or less been established.

Bishops assumed the authority of the apostles and played the central role in this regard. By the middle of the second century, everyone believed that the episcopal system had always been in operation and had been derived from the apostles themselves. Just as the early churches claimed whenever possible to be founded by an apostle, the bishops tried to establish lines of succession directly to the apostles which proved their claims to this derived authority.

Apostolic succession has been a point of contention throughout church history, especially since the Reformation. It is still a matter of contention between churches who claim authority through apostolic succession and those which claim the episcopal office cannot be established and only the New Testament is authoritative. At this very early date the groundwork was laid for subsequent controversies which have since been the excuse and the occasion for Christian division.

Christians began holding regular weekly meetings for worship, on the first day of the week, the day of the Lord's resurrection, in lieu of the Jewish Sabbath. They broke bread at the table of fellowship, repeating the actions of the Lord just prior to his death. The observance of this service was in response of Jesus' instructions to do it in memory of himself and it soon became the central rite in which all Christians engaged.

The importance of the Lord's Supper has never been lost. But where the Holy Communion was meant to be a great creative force for unity, it became the center of violent disagreement and dispute. The Messianic Banquet has taken a number of titles, all of which refer to the same basic act of worship: the Lord's Supper, the Mass, the Holy Eucharist, the Liturgy, etc. Differences of conviction have dealt with every aspect of the Banquet — its meaning, its language, its frequency, its ceremony — even whether leavened or unleavened bread should be used. All this has caused Christian division and it continues to do so. What is particularly ironic is that this sacramental rite, intended to express unity, continues to be an issue for division among Christians.

Other elements in Christian worship were borrowed from Jewish worship. The reading of sacred scriptures, singing of chants, teachings and prayers were adopted and modified more and more for Christian use. Even the Jewish religious observances were changed to fit the new Christian doctrines. The Passover became a time of remembrance of the death of Jesus, while the celebration of the Cleansing of the Temple became the remembrance of his birth.

The New Testament did not exist during the second century. The collection of books that make up the Canon of the New Testament had not yet been fixed. The Gospels and the letters of Paul were circulated as working documents among churches but only the Old Testament books were formerly recognized as Scripture. Not until the third century did the Gospels and the Pauline Epistles gain importance equal to the books of the Old Testament.

Sometime during the fourth century the Canon was fixed, providing a source of guidance for true faith and for the rejection of false doctrine. A movement developed within the church to drop the Old Testament books from the Canon! Disputes over the sacraments continued, such as the proper practice of Baptism. The nature of the Last Supper was disputed.

Another point of contention concerned the date Easter was to be observed. In Asia Minor, Easter was celebrated on the Jewish date of Nisan 14, on whichever day of the week it happened to fall. These followers claimed they derived the practice from St. John. In Rome, Easter was celebrated on the first Sunday following Nisan 14. The Roman practice prevailed. When Victor became Pope (A.D.189-198), he suppressed the former practice by threatening to excommunicate the bishop of Asia Minor if his followers did not cease their practice. Over a period of time, other discrepancies arose in the dates of feasts.

Until the end of the first century, Christianity was largely a Jewish way of thought. It was open to Gentiles and pagan converts but had not had to face the philosophical schools based on different thinking. The spread of Christianity through the Roman world made it necessary for Christians to justify their beliefs, especially as they came in contact with the learned world.

At first Jesus was preached as the man chosen by God, and whose approval had been sealed through his resurrection. He was shown to be a true Jew and to have fulfilled the prophecies of the Old Testament. But contact with the Greek world made different demands on Christianity. It is necessary to realize that when Jesus himself taught, he assumed religious and historical ideas which he never mentioned, simply because they were known by the Jewish religious at that time. Christian beliefs were not yet formed in a defined sense and attempts to relate them to current thought involved speculative theories. There was no way to reach an agreed truth except

192

through the exchange of ideas among thinkers.

Judaism had already been influenced by Greek spirit and Greek language in the Diaspora. In Palestine the eschatological hope was the resurrection of the dead. In the Diaspora, Jews believed in the Greek idea of the immortality of the soul. When Christianity spread throughout the empire, the eschatological and messianic expectation receded into the background. It was not possible for people in foreign lands to think of the appearance of a messiah who would restore the glory of the people of Israel. If they wanted to explain their religion to the intelligent members of the Roman society, they could not speak of a messiah. Instead of the expectation for the future of Israel, there appeared an expectation which pertained to the individual and his immortal soul.

The Gospel entered the empire as a joyful message and the power of the Spirit of God. The Gospel of Jesus originally was the message of Jesus. It was the message Jesus proclaimed about God and man. The early church made this Gospel into a message about Jesus. Unfortunately, the message of Jesus has been obscured. The chief elements of Jesus' message and the faith of Jesus were belief in the fatherhood of God, divine providence, the brotherhood of men — the children of God and the infinite value of the individual human being.

In the early twentieth century, Adolf von Harnack published his theory of the Hellenization of Christianity. The great historian of Christian dogma gave his lectures at the University of Berlin in 1899-1900 entitled, "The Essence of Christianity." His historical conclusions for his lectures were from his seven-volume series, *History of Dogma*, which he published in 1884.

Harnack believed that Christianity, which began as a movement within Judaism, was transformed at a very early date from this original Gospel into dogmatic Christianity. He distinguished an early period before Christianity, followed by a lengthly time during which dogma grew in the bosom of the church. Dogma was not a part of the original faith but developed later as a definite stage in the history of the church. It was the original Christian Gospel that provided the soil out of which dogma grew. "Dogma...in its conception and development," according to Harnack, "is a work of the Greek spirit on the soil of the Gospel."

Dogma developed within the Christian tradition. The Christianity of Justin Martyr in the middle of the second century, Clement of Alexandria at the end of the second century, or Origen in the middle of the third century is not the same Christianity of Mark or Paul in the first century, or the teachings of Jesus. Some of the differences are the development of fixed offices, such as bishops as channels of God's grace and signs; the conviction that man's relation to his God and Christ is dependent on an inspired book and divine rules of faith; the belief that faith in God is not enough but also one's intellectual assent to a body of doctrine.

Hellenic influences began toward the end of the first century but it wasn't until the third century that they became dominant in the Christian consciousness and within Christian institutions. Harnack did not originate the theory of the Hellenization of the Gospel but he has had such an enormous influence on Christian thinking that Hellenization is usually associated with his name. Harnack saw these developments within Christianity as corruptions or deviations from the original faith, or external changes that do not affect the basis of the faith.

The Christian religion, the religion of Jesus does not change. It does not *become* anything over the course of history. Christianity is defined *as it was in the beginning*. The message of Jesus is the message of Israel. The God who raised Jesus from the dead is the God of Abraham, Isaac and Jacob; He is also the God of the faithful remnant that continues on — they are the Remnant of Israel, the True Israel, the New Covenant.

"He who testifies to these things says, 'Surely I am coming soon.' Amen. Come, Lord Jesus!

"The grace of the Lord Jesus be with all. Amen" (Rev.22:20-21).

194

Abbreviations

QS	The Manual of Discipline (Serek ha-yahad)
CD	The Damascus Document (Coventers of Damascus)
QM	The War Between the Sons of Light and the Sons of Darkness (Milhama)
MR	The Messianic Rule
QHAB	Commentary on Habakkuk
Deut.	Deuteronomy
Jer.	Jeremiah
Mt.	Matthew
Mk.	Mark
Lk.	Luke
Jn.	John
Acts	Acts of the Apostles
1 Jn.	1 John
2 Jn.	2 John
3 Jn.	3 John
Rev.	Revelation
Antiq.	The Jewish Antiquities

Notes

Chapter 1. The Dead Sea Scrolls

1. Wady is Arabic for a watercourse, which may be a raging torrent after a thunderstorm, but usually is bone dry.

2. Kahil Iskander Shaheen, called "Kando," possessed the "Temple" or "Torah" scroll as late as 1967 when it was obtained by Yigael Yadin of the Hebrew University.

3. The monastery is believed to be the site of the house of St. Mark's mother, the house Peter went to after his miraculous release from prison.

4. Father of famed archaeologist, Yigael Yadin.

5. Dr. Sukenik defended his scroll findings as authentic even though he would not come to believe it himself until three years later.

6. R. de Vaux, director of the French School of Archaeology in Jerusalem.

7. It is to the everlasting credit of the Jordan Government that, pressed as they were by their own demands, they voted to preserve the library which was of crucial importance to Christians and Jews but of minor interest to Moslems.

8. A university in Hanover, Germany.

Chapter 2. Khirbet Qumran

1. Khirbet: ruins.

2. The Manual of Discipline (Serek ha-yahad).

3. Potsherds were used in the ancient world as one today uses scraps of paper for scribbling or making memoranda.

4. R. de Vaux, *Archaeology and the Dead Sea.*

Chapter 3. Battle of the Scrolls

1. According to the Damascus Document and the commentar-

ies, the founder of the group is the Teacher of Righteousness or the Righteous Teacher, a greatly revered individual who has profoundly influenced the organization and spirituality of the Community.

2. R. de Vaux, *Archaeology and the Dead Sea.*
3. R. de Vaux, *Archaeology and the Dead Sea.*
4. R. de Vaux, *Archaeology and the Dead Sea.*
5. R. de Vaux, *Archaeology and the Dead Sea.*

Chapter 4. Exile in Babylon

1. *2 Kings 24:8-15,* "...and Nebuchadnezzar, king of Babylon, came against the city and his servants did besiege it...and he carried away all Jerusalem...And he carried away Jehoiachim and his family to Babylon."
2. *2 Kings 25:1-2,* "...Nebuchadnezzar, king of Babylon, came...And the city was besieged unto the eleventh year of Zedekiah."
3. *2 Kings 25:7.*
4. *2 Kings 25:26; Jeremiah 43:7.*
5. *Hosea 12:7; Amos 8:5-6,* "He is a merchant, the balances of deceit are in his hand: he loveth to oppress."
6. Werner Keller, *The Bible as History.*
7. 605-562 B.C.
8. Werner Keller, *The Bible as History.*

Chapter 5. Return to the Promise Land

1. *Zechariah 1:1,* "the eighth month of the second year of Darius" (Oct.-Nov., 520 B.C.). *Ezra 6:15,* "the third day of the month of Adar, in the sixth year of Darius" (12 Mar., 515 B.C.).
2. *Zechariah 9:3-4,* "And Tyrus did build herself a stronghold and heaped up silver as the dust and fine gold as the mire of the streets. Behold, the Lord will cast her out and he will smite her power in the sea."
3. *Zechariah 9:5,* "...Gaza shall...be very sorrowful."
4. 1 *Maccabees 1:15.*

200

5. G. Vermes, *The Dead Sea Scrolls in English*, The Hasidim included a strong priestly element descended from the Zadokite pontifical dynasty which held supreme power in the Temple of Jerusalem from the time of Solomon to that of Antiochus Epiphanes.

6. *2 Maccabees 5:16*, "And taking the holy vessels with polluted hands, and with profane hands putting down the things that were dedicated by other kings to the augmentation and glory and honor of the place he gave them away."

7. *1 Maccabees 1:44*, "And the king sent letters by the hand of messengers unto Jerusalem and the cities of Judah, that they should follow laws strange to the land."

8. *1 Maccabees 1:63*, "...many chose rather to die, that they might not be defiled."

9. *Amos 5:26-27*, This passage contains a divine threat: the Israelites would take themselves and their idols into exile. "You shall take up Sakkuth your king and Kaiwar your star-god, your images which you made for yourselves, for I will take you into exile beyond Damascus." The Damascus Document (Coventers of Damascus) transforms this threat into a promise of salvation by changing certain words and omitting others. The text reads: "I will exile the tabernacle of your king and the bases of your statues from my tent to Damascus."

Chapter 6. The Hasmonean Dynasty

1. *1 Maccabees 2:1-25*.
2. *1 Maccabees 4:36*.
3. *Damascus Document I*.
4. *Commentary on Habakkuk*.
5. *Damascus Document IX:28*, The Hasidim viewed themselves as the True Israel and the Pharisees as a sect.
6. *Commentary on Habakkuk IX; Commentary on Nahum*.
7. David Flusser, *Messianic Belief Among the Jews*.
8. *Commentary on Nahum*.
9. *Commentary on Nahum I:6-7*.

Chapter 7. Life Under the Romans

1. *Mark 5:20, 7:31; Matthew 4:25.*
2. Edward Lohse, *New Testament Environment.*
3. Herod died in 4 B.C.
4. *Matthew 2:22, 14:9; Mark 6:14.*
5. *Matthew 2:22.*
6. *Luke 3:1.*

Chapter 8. The Community of Qumran

1. Eschatology is the name given to the doctrine of Last things such as Judgment, Heaven and Hell.
2. John Marco Allegro, *The Mystery of the Dead Sea Scrolls Revealed.*
3. *Damascus Document XIII.*
4. The Zadok Priesthood had presided over all of the synagogues in the Diaspora when they controlled the Temple.
5. Magen Broshi, *Essenes and Early Christianity.*
6. The New Covenant is not a second covenant which has replaced the first one. Rather, it is the covenant which God made with Israel in the Sinai and which now, at the End of Days, has been reinstituted.
7. R. de Vaux, *Archaeology and the Dead Sea Scrolls.*
8. Josephus spent one year of initiation into the Essene Church and became a member of the Essene movement. He used this lesson to save himself after his capture by the Romans when he prophesied Vespasian would someday become Emperor.
9. Bargil Pixner, *An Essene Quarter on Mount Zion*, close to the ancient First Wall, now south of the Turkish Zion Gate.
10. Bargil Pixner, *The Essenes of Jerusalem.*

Chapter 9. Scrolls of the Community

1. The word "sect" is most often used to denote a group in a derogatory manner. The group at Qumran did not view themselves as a sect but rather as the legitimate heirs to Israel's

202

Priesthood, the rightful Jewish descendents of Zadok.

2. Apocryphal works are "hidden" works; it can be taken to mean the works were rejected or suppressed or that the authors intended their meaning to be cryptic.

3. Pseudepigraphal works are a well known genre in Jewish literature – writings in which later writers speak through the mouth of a patriarch or prophet.

4. The oldest document that is credited to have been written (produced) by the Priesthood.

5. The Levites occupied in Hebrew theocracy a position midway between the Priesthood and the people.

6. *Matthew 5:33-37.*

7. At the End of Times, each person would be given a final chance to join on the side of good before the final line was drawn.

8. As opposed to the forced conversion under Aristobulus.

9. Beginning the day of rest, no more work shall be done after the time "when the disc of the sun is the distance of its diameter from the Gate of Hope" *(CD XI:13-14).*

Chapter 10. Second Battle of the Scrolls

1. Dupont-Sommer believed Jesus to be the same man who founded the Community and placed Jesus' life one hundred years earlier than generally believed.

2. *Commentary on Nahum.*

3. *Commentary on Nahum.*

Chapter 11. Gospel Writers

1. Although several Christian theologians raised interesting questions about the authorship of the Gospels early on, critical study did not begin until the Enlightenment of the Eighteenth Century.

2. Roman records uncovered through archaeology along with indirect rabbinical sources show that Jesus was crucified by the Romans.

3. David Flusser, *Messianic Belief Among the Jews.*

4. *The Messianic Rule.*

5. Donald Juel, *New Testament Literature.*

6. Matthew's emphasis on the proper behavior for a community of believers presupposes the existence of some sort of institutionalized church.

Chapter 12. The Gospel According to John

1. A system of mystical religious and philosophical doctrines, combining Christianity with Greek and Oriental philosophies, propagated by early Christian sects that were denounced as heretical.

2. Zoroaster founded the national religion of the Persians about 600 B.C. His influence was widespread from India to the shores of the Mediterranean.

3. Ramond E. Brown, *The Qumran Scrolls and the Johannine Gospel and Epistles,* Zoroastrian religion taught a dualism where the forces of good and evil, led by Ahura Mazda and Angra Mainyu, respectively, are engaged in an ethical combat. It is a struggle between truth and deceit, light and darkness. It also is eschatological, for ultimately the triumph of Ahura Mazda is envisaged. One great difference separates John's dualism and that of Qumran from Zoroastrianism. In Zoroastrianism the good and evil spirits coexist as gods; two independent, uncreated forces. The imported dualism of Qumran has been influenced by the Old Testament theology of God the Creator who has created both forces.

4. Yigael Yadin, *The Temple Scroll,* "most scholars are in agreement – rightly so, in my opinion – that the influence of the Community's teachings is recognizable in the views, practices, ideology and even the very phraseology of the founders of Christianity."

5. Frank Moore Cross, *The Ancient Library of Qumran and Modern Biblical Studies,* "The Essene parallels to John and the Johannine Epistles will come as a surprise only to those students of John who have attempted to read John as a work under strong Greek influence. It now turns out – as a small coterie of scholars

204

have long maintained – that John has its strongest affinities not with the Greek world, or Philonic Judaism, but with Palestinian Judaism. Its concepts of truth, knowledge, spirit, and even the Word must be seen, not as rooted in Greek or Gnostic thought, but as concepts emerging precisely out of Sectarian Judaism. So rather than being the most Hellenistic of the Gospels, John now proves to be the most Jewish."

6. John's Gospel is addressed to the disciples of John the Baptist (Essaeic followers) and Jewish members of the Essene Church as well as others in the Jewish milieu. The tension between John and the Essene Priesthood and their practices manifests itself beyond anything else in the New Testament.

7. C.H. Dodd, *Historical Tradition in the Fourth Gospel.*

8. R.T. Fortna, *The Gospel of Signs.*

9. The Synoptic Gospels are difficult to reconcile wherein during his ministry, Jesus goes only once to Jerusalem in the last days of his life.

10. In present day historical and theological studies, it is generally accepted that John wrote the three Epistles although the first Church Fathers believed that he composed only the first Epistle.

Chapter 13. Messianic Age

1. Since the time of the Exile a strong Jewish community had lived in Babylon, and many had taken up residence in Syria for reasons of trade and commerce. Jewish communities flourished in Asia Minor and North Africa. In Egypt alone, the number of Jews exceeded one million (Philo "In Flaccum" XLIII), a large part living in Alexandria. There were also smaller Jewish localities such as Cyrenia and the Roman military colony Philippi (Acts 16:13).

2. Edward Lohse, *The Political History of Judaism in the Hellenistic Period,* pluralism during this time not only included differing beliefs in Judaism but was also influenced to varying degrees by Roman paganism and Hellenistic influence.

3. Morton Smith – the Pharisees were the smallest of all of the

denominations during this time. Because they were one of two groups to survive the destruction of Jerusalem and the War with Rome (the other being Christianity) does not make them the normative group of the period.

4. *Exodus 21:2-3; Leviticus 25:39-41.*

5. The Hasidim had, during their control of the Priesthood in Jerusalem, been the head of all the synagogues in the Diaspora. When the Pharisees gained control of the Temple, many of the synagogues naturally gravitated to them.

6. John Marco Allegro, *The Treasure of the Copper Scroll.*

7. John Marco Allegro, *The Mystery of the Dead Sea Scrolls Revealed,* "In one of their hymns, the Community pictures itself as a pregnant woman suffering the pangs of parturition as she gives birth to her 'firstborn,' who is described in terms reminiscent of the Child of Isaiah IX:6, the 'Wonderful Counsellor.' Most scholars agree that the passage retains its biblical messianic significance, in which case it appears that the Community believed that out of its suffering of atonement for 'the land' would come the Annointed One or Christ."

8. Werner Keller, *The Star of Bethlehem.*

9. Donald Juel, *New Testament Literature*, Matthew characterizes almost every incident he relates in the beginning of his book as a fulfillment of a specific biblical prophecy. The thrust of these traditional associations is quite clear. It provides striking testimony to the importance of the hero.

10. Yigael Yadin, *The Temple Scroll*, "This special calendar is the calendar of the Books of Jubilees and Enoch, two of the so-called pseudepigraphal works. This fact, I believe, supports the theory, which more and more scholars have come to accept, that Jubilees and similar pseudepigraphal writings are compositions embodying the teachings of a wider movement from which the Qumran Community developed in the course of time."

11. Yigael Yadin, *The Temple Scroll*, "With all the grave implications of different calendars, the prime issue, irrespective of which calendar was followed, was over the day of the month on which the Pentecost was to be celebrated. This was the subject of controversy within Judaism from time immemorial."

12. *Damascus Document VI*, "The feasts and the Day of Fasting must be kept according to the finding of the members of the New Covenant."

13. Yigael Yadin, *The Temple Scroll*, "Since the Community was cut off from the Temple, they may have held their substitute ceremonies at Qumran at the appointed times. The original Hebrew term that is translated into English as 'times appointed' or 'appointed times' was subject to divergent interpretations. Our author [of The Temple Scroll] clearly understood it to mean fixed times. In so doing, he broke with the interpretation by normative Judaism, at least according to the Mishnah, which held the meaning to be 'at various times throughout the year.' "

14. Yigael Yadin, *The Temple Scroll*, "There is now a near consensus that the earliest of such relations (early Christianity and the Community at Qumran) emerged in the time of John the Baptist. From all we know through the New Testament – and there is very little, for the stories associated with him are brief, and heavily edited – it seems evident that John himself not only knew the Essenes but had been a member of the Community."

15. In scroll P72 it says that it was "God the Christ" who delivered the people out of Egypt and other ancient manuscripts say that it was "Jesus" who "saved his people" and led the children out of Egypt into Israel. The Essene priesthood believed the Messiah of Israel would return and "deliver his people."

16. John's baptism was a departure from Essene baptism to that time. John offered a final chance to the masses to join on the side of God before the final line was drawn at the End of Days.

17. In *The Manual of Discipline,* it is stated that a man cannot be sanctified from sin by seas and rivers nor purified by any water for washing, but only "by the Holy Spirit, in His truth, shall he be cleansed of all his iniquities."

18. It may be that the mention of the "beloved disciple" serves to identify a particular authority of the author.

19. The Gospel *John* consistently claims Moses and Jewish tradition as witnesses for Jesus *(5:39-47, 8:56-58, 12:37-42).*

20. C.H. Dodd, *The Founder of Christianity*, Jesus is being depicted in a controversy with this *devil.* He counters each

challenge with a quotation from Deuteronomy. It is in Deuter-onomy where Moses addressed the Israelites toward the end of their wandering in the wilderness:

"Remember all the road by which the Lord your God led you these forty years in the wilderness, to humble you and put you to the test, to see whether you were minded to keep his commandments or not. He humbled you and famished you with hunger, and then fed you with manna, which your fathers never knew, to teach you that man cannot live on bread alone, but lives on every word that God utters."

And in Matthew:

"Jesus was led away by the Spirit into the wilderness to be tested by the devil. For forty days and nights he fasted, and at the end of them he was famished. The tempter approached him an said 'If you are the Son of God, tell these stones to become bread.' Jesus answered, 'Scripture says, "Man cannot live on bread alone; he lives on every word that God utters."'"

21. Here this *devil* is even able to quote from the scriptures *(Psalms 91:11-12)*, verbatim.

22. The crowds had gathered beside the sea at Qumran for the celebration of the Passover.

Chapter 14. The Ministry of Jesus

1. The tribe of Judah was geographically located in the King-dom of Judah, the Southern Kingdom, and the territories of the eleven other tribes were located in the Northern Kingdom, the Kingdom of Israel (Galilee).

2. K. Stendahl, ed., *The Scrolls and the New Testament*, "The Sermon on the Mount and the Qumran Texts," from the Austrian scholar Professor Kurt Schubert, who was the first to elaborate on this theme.

3. Messiah – the King of Israel.

4. Scholars believe that one of the main themes of the Gospels is the ongoing opposition between Jesus and the Pharisees, when perhaps, the real clash and the main thrust of his ministry was directed toward the Essene Priesthood, their interpretation of

the Mosaic Law, their eschatological hatred and the belief of their followers, the Essene Church. It is not coincidental that many of Jesus' teachings and actions happen to be aimed directly at Essene thought: his personal contact with the diseased and physically handicapped, his acceptance of women and children into his presence, forgiveness for sin, his instructions to "love one's enemy" and to "carry the Roman soldier's pack the extra mile," his promise that "the least shall be made first," etc.

5. Josephus, *Antiguities, XVIII,* where the Gospels in referring to Herod Antipas' episode, chose to emphasize the moral charge that the Baptist brought against the ruler, Josephus, who may be a more reliable witness, stresses the political fear aroused. Instead of John being arrested because of his criticism of Herod's unorthodox marriage, his downfall was caused by his and/or others' political aims.

6. Jesus being warned by the Pharisees is one of the great inconsistencies of the Gospels. Perhaps Jesus is warned by the Levites, the priests of the Community.

7. It is argued that for Jesus to be in a position to cleanse the temple Precincts, he had to have public status as a prophet and also a numerous following. It may be that this following consisted of an "Angel of the Lord," an Essene bodyguard; a group of his followers dedicated to the protection of the Messiah of Israel.

8. Dr. B. Mazar, *Mountain of the Lord,* Mazar has excavated and described in detail the Hanuyot of the Temple Mount and its vast substructures. The Temple Mount was erected over the south, east and west slopes of the Mount Moriah. The slopes beneath are filled by stone vaults and halls beneath the southeastern part of the platform of the Temple Mount. They are known as the "Solomon Stables" and along them ran the subterranean passages which led from the Double and Triple Hulda Gates to the surface platform. This was Herod's Royal Portico, the three-storied and colonnaded edifices known as the Hanuyot.

9. V.E. Epstein, *The Historicity of the Gospel Account of the Cleansing of the Temple,* Caiaphas had allowed rival merchants to set up animal stalls in the Temple confines.

10. During the days of Pontius Pilate, "the Sanhedrin had been

expelled... (from the chamber of Hewn Stone, consecrated ground), and took its seat at the Hanuyot" (*Sanhedrin 41:2; Aboda Zora 8:2*). Certain activities were transferred and reorganized. The reorganization also allowed dealers in ritual objects to operate in the lower sections. This relaxed attitude was characteristic of ancient Greek public places.

11. It is possible that these modernizing trends infuriated the more puritanical people who saw the change in the Hanuyot as an unbecoming intrusion of business into the areas of worship. The Essenes held that the Hanuyot was part of the Temple proper and therefore sacred. The Gospels take it for granted that Jesus' action was called for, without giving any explanation of just what motivated it.

12. John gives a glimpse of contemporary conditions of which the later Gospel writers were unaware (*Jn. 2:13-22*). Modern New Testament scholars are past the stage which considered that John's testimony lacks historicity. He is regarded as one of the main contemporary sources on early Christian background. It is John's reference to the very magnitude of Jesus' cleansing of the Hanuyot, especially of cattle and sheep, which throws new light on the varied functions and divisions of the Hanuyot at the different levels of this vast structure.

13. R.E. Brown, *Anchor Bible, pp. 114-125; Acts 6, 7:47-48.*

14. Donald Juel, *New Testament Literature, pp. 106-112.*

15. Jesus' crucifixion was his final message to his followers that he would not be the militant leader they had expected him to be.

16. Judas was the "Overseer" for the immediate followers of Jesus, an office which combined the responsibility for the matters of administration like work and finance. He controlled the purse and made expenditures on behalf of the entire group. He may have been the appropriate choice to initiate the final step to usher in the End of Days because he was the leader of the tribe of Judah, the tribe of King David, and his standing among the other disciples, the leaders of the other tribes, was very great. Who better to initiate the final action than the leader of the House of Judah?

17. *Sanhedrin 4:1.*

18. *Sanhedrin 4:1.*
19. Bargil Pixner, *An Essene Quarter on Mount Zion.*
20. Caiphas gave voice to a common sense maxim of political expedience. He was anxious to take care of Jesus lest the Romans take action against the Jews. He could not expect that Jesus would die not in the place of Israel, but on behalf of "the True Israel."
21. *John 18:31.*
22. Paul Winter, *On the Trial of Jesus.*

Chapter 15. The Aftermath

1. B. Pixner, M. Broshi and others believe there is an irrefutable link between the Essenes and the early Christians. Some believe that Paul met a group or a community of Essenes, "an Angel of the Lord," on his fateful journey to Damascus.

2. *Damascus Document B, II; VII,* the Community expected the Messianic Age to begin forty years after the death of their Righteous Teacher when he would return as the "Sceptre," the "Prince of the Whole Congregation," their King-Messiah.

3. The sixth month of the Jewish year is Elul. J.T. Milik reports that the Essene yearly cycle included seven principal feasts, each following the previous at intervals of seven weeks. These feasts corresponded in general to similar feasts in normative Judaism. There was one additional feast he believed to be their Feast of Feasts, the Renewal of the Covenant. Yigael Yadin writes from *The Temple Scroll,* "To judge by the rites of its celebration, it was undoubtedly the most important of all. While the others were to be observed for only one day, this was to last six days; and throughout this six-day feast, each of the twelve tribes, two per day, was to bring a burnt offering to the Lord. I am inclined to believe it most likely that it began on Monday the 23rd of Elul...the detailed instructions in the Mishnah show quite clearly that in normative tradition there was no single festival, let alone a major one like that described in the Temple Scroll." On the Feast of Renewal, some forty years after the crucifixion of the Teacher, they initiated their offensive. For the first time in two

hundred years the Temple came into the hands of the Sons of Light, the Zadokite Priesthood.

4. At the time of the Second War (A.D. 132-5), Simon bar Kosebah who led the Jewish uprising against Rome was believed by his followers to be the messiah, the Prince of Israel. His followers knew him as "Bar Kochebah" which means "Son of the Star," and on the other hand by his enemies who ridiculed his pretentions as "Bar Kozebah," which means "Son of the Lie." During the War of 66, John of Gischala was never perceived as the messiah. The Zealots believed the messiah would resurrect to join in the battle.

5. Yigael Yadin, *Masada, Herod's Fortress and the Zealot's Last Stand.*

6. The Sadducees did not maintain synagogues in the Diaspora. Their power center was the Temple, and when Jerusalem fell, their fate was sealed as well. The reconstruction of the Jewish communities fell to the Pharisees.

7. *Luke 6:22; John 9:22, 12:42, 16:2.*

Chapter 16. One Final Word

1. John Marco Allegro, *The Mystery of the Dead Sea Scrolls Revealed*, "It has been suggested by others that the office of 'Bishop' in the Church has its origin in the Qumran 'Overseer.' The general Superintendent was responsible for matters of admimistration like work and finance, and there was similarly an Overseer in each 'camp' who combined with these executive duties the guidance and instruction of candidates for initiation. This curious combination of administration and religious duties is found again in the *episkopos* or Bishop of the early Christian Church."

Selected Bibliography

Aland, K.	*Synopsis of the Four Gospels*	(New York, 1982)
Albright, W.F.,	*The Archaeology of Palestine*	(New York, 1960)
Allegro, J.M.,	*Dead Sea Scrolls*	(New York, 1956)
	The Treasure of the Copper Scroll	(New York, 1960)
Black, M.,	*The Scrolls and Christian Origins*	(New York, 1961)
	The Scrolls and Christianity	(London, 1969)
Brownlee, W.H.,	*The Dead Sea Manual of Discipline* (Oxford, 1951)	
Burrows, M.,	*The Dead Sea Scrolls*	(New York, 1955)
	More Light on the Dead Sea Scrolls (New York, 1958)	
Cornfeld, G.,	*Daniel to Paul: Jews in Conflict with Graeco-Roman Civilization* (New York, 1981)	
	The Historical Jesus: A Scholarly View to the Man and His World (New York, 1983)	
Cross, F.M.,	*The Ancient Library of Qumran and Biblical Studies* (London, 1958)	
Davies, A.P.,	*The Meaning of the Dead Sea Scrolls* (New York, 1956)	
Dodd, C.H.,	*The Old Testament in the New*	(New York, 1968)
	The Founder of Christianity	(New York, 1970)

213

Dupont-Sommer, A.,

        The Dead Sea Scrolls   (London, 1952)

        The Jewish Sect of Qumran and the Essenes
        (London, 1955)

        The Essene Writings from Qumran (Oxford, 1961)

Flusser, D.   *Aspects of the Dead Sea Scrolls*   (London, 1958)

Fritsch, C.T.,   *The Qumran Community*   (Buffalo, 1956)

Gaster, T.H.,   *The Scriptures of the Dead Sea Sect*
                                  (London, 1957)

Harnack, A. Von,

        What Is Christianity   (Folcroft, 1978)

Hengel, M.,   *Judaism and Hellenism*   (New York, 1961)

Josephus,   *The Jewish War*

        The Jewish Antiquities

Juel, D.,   *New Testament Literature*   (New York, 1978)

Keller, W.,   *The Bible as History*   (New York, 1981)

Lohse, E.,   *The New Testament Environment* (Nashville, 1976)

MacMullen, R., *Christianizing the Roman Empire* (Yale, 1984)

Milik, J.T.,   *Ten Years of Discovery in the Wilderness of Judea*
                                  (London, 1959)

Mowry, L.,   *The Dead Sea Scrolls and the Early Church*
                                  (New York, 1962)

Pagels, E.,   *The Gnostic Gospels*   (New York, 1981)

Pliny,   *Naturalis Historia*

Ploeg, J. Vander,

The Excavations at Qumran (New York, 1958)

Rowley, H.H., *From Moses to Qumran* (Salem, 1963)

Sanders, J.A., *The Dead Sea Psalms Scroll* (New York, 1967)

Schweitzer, A., *The Quest of the Historical Jesus* (New York, 1968)

Stendahl, K., *The Scrolls and the New Testament*
(London, 1958)

Sutcliffe, E.F., *The Monks of Qumran* (New York, 1960)

Trever, J.C., *The Discovery of the Scrolls* (New York, 1950)

Vaux, R. de, *Archaeology and the Dead Sea Scrolls*
(London, 1973)

Vermes, G., *Discovery in the Judean Desert* (London, 1956)

The Dead Sea Scrolls in English (London, 1962)

The Dead Sea Scrolls: Qumran in Perspective
(London, 1977)

Waddams, H.M.,
The Struggle for Christian Unity (New York, 1971)

Wilken, R.L., *The Myth of Christian Beginnings*
(Notre Dame, 1980)

Wilson, E. *The Scrolls From the Dead Sea* (London, 1955)

Yadin, Y. *The Temple Scroll* (New York, 1985)

Index

Jordan River, 1, 5, 22, 37, 39, 40, 107, 109, 123, 125, 127, 129, 133, 135-137, 146, 155, 176
Joseph (Mary's Husband), 39, 115, 116, 119, 123
Joseph of Arimathea, 162
Josephus, Flavius, 42, 44, 46, 48, 112, 114, 124, 127, 141, 142, 146, 157, 175-177, 179, 181, 183
Joshua, 1
Jotapota, 176
Judas Iscariot, 136, 153, 154, 159, 162
Judas Maccabaeus, 31-33
Judas the Galilean, 40
Jupiter, 117, 118
Justin, 194

Kando, 3
Kepler, J., 117, 118, 126
Kiln, 11, 16
Kittim, 67
Kuhn, K.G., 97, 100

Land of Damascus, 29, 61-63, 105, 106, 120, 133
Last Supper, 48, 92, 128, 130, 157, 159, 191, 192
Levites, 51, 52, 61, 66, 70, 122, 174
Library, 7
Ligatures, 14
Linen Wrappings, 15
Luke, Gospel of Saint, 89-95, 101, 106, 114, 115, 126, 127, 129, 130, 135, 138, 141, 145, 148, 149, 157, 160, 166, 168
Luke, Saint, 90, 93, 95, 114, 116, 124, 128, 129, 138, 139, 187, 188

Maccabean Revolt, 31, 32, 40, 110
Machaerus, 146
Magi, 116, 119, 123
Mandate, 3, 4
Manual of Discipline, 5, 41, 50-60, 95, 101-105, 120, 121, 125, 140-143, 157, 173
Marianne, 38

Marianne, Tower of , 183
Mark, Gospel of Saint, 89-95, 106, 114, 138, 145, 148, 153, 156, 157, 161, 163, 173
Mark, Saint, 93, 94, 128, 146, 194
Mary, 39, 115, 116, 119, 123
Masada, 40, 184
Masoretic Test, 4
Mattaniah, 20
Mattathias, 31, 40
Matthew, Gospel of Saint, 89-95, 106, 114, 116, 117, 127, 132, 138-145, 147, 148
Matthew, Saint, 90, 93-95, 118, 119, 128, 138, 139, 143, 146
Medes, 23
Mediterranean, 110, 118
Menahem, 40, 48
Messianic Movement (Messianism), 34, 50, 90, 91, 108, 115-117, 122, 124, 125, 127, 133, 136, 137, 147, 153, 158, 159, 166, 167, 173, 185, 193
Messianic Rule (Banquet), 47, 50, 79-81, 91, 122, 123, 133, 156, 159, 172, 173, 191
Metropolitan of St. Mark's, 3, 4
Milik, J.T., 7, 10, 12, 14, 16
Mishnah, 158
Modin, 31
Moses, 21, 26, 33, 41, 45, 47, 50, 51, 55, 60, 84, 90, 95, 109, 111, 119, 121, 124, 125, 131-133, 139, 140, 145, 169, 172, 186, 188, 189
Muhammed the Wolf, 2
Murabba'at, 6, 14, 15

Nabataean, 29
Nabonidus, 23
Nahum, 50, 86
Nash Papyrus, 4 ,14
Nazarene, (Nazareth), 123, 149, 159, 171, 185, 186
Nebuchadnezzar, 20-23, 61
Nero, 168, 171, 172, 176, 177
Nicodemus, 136, 162

Ptolemies II, 26
Ptolemies IV, 27, 34

"Q" (Quelle), 89, 93, 139
Quirinius, P. Sulpicius, 116

Refectory, 157, 158
Reformation, 190
Remnant, 41, 61, 68, 169, 194
Resurrection, 34, 137, 191-193
Rome, 35-40, 43, 44, 48, 109, 111, 160, 168, 171, 172, 175-177, 183, 184, 186, 190, 192

Sadducees, 33, 34, 38, 40, 84, 111, 163, 184
Samaria, 39, 40, 109, 110, 130, 133, 136, 168, 170
Samaritan, the Good, 2
Sanhedrin, 137, 149, 155, 156, 158-160, 165
Saturn, 117, 118
Saturnius, 116
Saul, King, 1
Schnabel, P., 117
Schubert, K., 124
Schweitzer, A., 154
Scriptio Plena, 14
Scriptorium, 11, 12, 87
Second Jewish War, 17
Sepphoris, 38
Septuagint, 27
Shema, 185
Shewbread, Table of the, 183
Shrine of Books, 4
Simon Bar Giora, 176, 178, 183
Simon Bar Kokhba, 17
Simon Maccabaeus, 32-34
Sippar, 117, 118
Skehan, P.W., 7
Solomon, 39, 143, 164

Speleologists, 6
Starcky, J., 7
Stephen, the martyr, 170
Strugnell, J., 7, 14
Sukenik, E.L., 3, 5, 15, 72
Synoptic (Synopsis), 89, 92, 93, 97, 98, 105-107, 126, 128, 129, 149, 156, 157

Ta'amireh Bedouin, 2, 3, 6-8
Tacitus, 183
Teacher of Righteousness, 13, 32, 61, 63, 72, 84-86, 102, 103, 129, 130, 138, 172, 173
Temple, Rebuilding, 24, 39
Temple of Peace, 184
Ten Cities, 37
Tetrarch, 39, 126
Thanksgiving Hymns, 5, 50, 72-79, 127
Therapeute, 123
Tiberias, 38
Tiberius, Caesar, 126, 160, 170
Titus, 42, 161, 176-179, 181-183
Trever, J.C., 4, 14
Tyre, 25
Tyrian coins, 164

United Nations, 3
Unity, 21, 42, 55, 84, 91, 189, 191
Upper Room, 48, 158, 168
Ur, 24

Vale of Achor, 47, 48
Vaux, R. de, 6, 7, 10, 12, 17
Vermes, G., 50, 61, 67, 72, 79, 112
Vespasian, Titus Flavius, 44, 176, 177, 184
Victor, Pope, 192
Vincent, L.H., 161